LIBRARY
LAS VEGAS REVIEW JOURNAL
P.O. BOX 70
LAS VEGAS, NEVADA 89125-0070

Howard Hughes, His Other Empire, and His Man

Howard Hughes, His Other Empire, and His Man

Clint Baxter and Jim Haworth

Drawings by Jim Haworth

VANTAGE PRESS
New York

FIRST EDITION

All rights reserved, including the right of
reproduction in whole or in part in any form.

Copyright © 1996 by Clint Baxter and Jim Haworth

Published by Vantage Press, Inc.
516 West 34th Street, New York, New York 10001

Manufactured in the United States of America
ISBN: 0-533-11696-1

Library of Congress Catalog Card No.: 95-90746

0 9 8 7 6 5 4 3 2 1

To our wives

To Iris Leavitt Haworth, my loving wife for over fifty years
Jim Haworth

To Helen Munn Baxter, my loving wife for over fifty years
Clint Baxter

Contents

Acknowledgments ix
The Book xi
Introduction xiii

Prologue 1
1. Early Story of Warm Springs Ranch 7
2. The Early Life and Trials of James S. Haworth 17
3. Howard Hughes's Younger Years 26
4. The War Years 52
5. The Fifties—The Decade of Stress 72
6. Hughes and TWA 83
7. Gold Butte 94
8. The Gold Mines 102
9. A Dream Comes True—Howard Hughes Buys Warm Springs 129
10. The Warm Springs Ranch and Hughes's Executives' Involvement During Hughes's Self-Imposed Asylum 149
11. Paranoia in the Seventies 195

Epilogue 213

Acknowledgments

We wish to give proper credit for citations and information from the many Howard Hughes publications written before and after his death; also, the contemporaries who grew up with and worked for Howard Hughes's organization, sharing personally and in writing their knowledge of Howard Hughes.

We also wish to acknowledge the true Hughes executives who worked with Jim Haworth and Iris Haworth to build the utopian Hughes's other empire for Howard Hughes.

The Church of Latter-Day Saints, Salt Lake City, Utah, provided access to the Hughes mansion for photographs and information.

Clark County Library, Las Vegas, was most helpful in providing material

The Clark County clerk provided copies of recorded deeds and transfers.

The few we met who had restricted personal access to Howard Hughes were most generous with interviews.

Much gratitude is given to Betsy Rogers, of Crestline, California, for her untiring days and weeks of typing, reworking, word-processing advice, and letter writing.

Nevada ranchers and neighbors of the Howard Hughes Warm Springs Ranch have been and are yet providing stories of Howard Hughes' other empire and Jim Haworth.

The Book

This volume is a narration of the rough and tough Warm Springs Ranch's early history together with original drawings by Jim Haworth, Howard Hughes's man of the empire. Jim, seventy-six years old in 1995, grew up in the Moapa Valley, Nevada, on the location of Howard Hughes's Warm Springs Ranch. Jim grew to manhood fighting the perils of the awesome Nevada desert. He relates hands-on experiences dealing with Hughes's property purchases, managing the ranch empire and being the cow boss, raising and showing horses and cattle for Howard Hughes and dealing with the Moapa Indians. Howard Hughes's awesome million acres of ranch and range were a challenge for Jim's ranching ego when he met monthly with Hughes's executives at 7000 Romaine Street, Los Angeles, Hughes's headquarters. Jim Haworth relates his close involvement in Howard Hughes's life and later settlement of Howard Hughes's estate.

The authors present interesting true stories of some of Howard Hughes's other lives not heretofore presented. Each chapter contains stories of eras in Howard Hughes's life and of Jim Haworth and the Hughes Warm Springs empire.

Graphic drawings by coauthor Jim Haworth were made on the scene during hair-raising events confronting Jim and his cowboys as they fought the elements on Howard Hughes's million-acre other empire.

Howard Hughes, His Other Empire, and His Man was coauthored by Clint Baxter, who did the Howard Hughes's life research, coordinated with Jim Haworth, who wrote the other empire stories and provided photos and drawings.

Several of Jim Haworth's drawings are included with his ranch stories. These were done by Jim, without art training, while he crouched at the evening campfire in the far reaches of the Hughes Warm Springs empire. It is concluded that Howard Hughes intended to retire to his six-bedroom, six-bath mansion and enjoy solitary bliss on his million-acre paradise.

Introduction

This is the true story of Howard Hughes and Jim Haworth, the man of Hughes's other empire and the man who nearly saved him. The authors introduce the reader to the real genetic character of Howard Hughes and his brilliant deeds resultant from inherited influences.

Howard Hughes was considered a genius by many, but his wisdom and determination were the determining factors in his amazing accomplishments. Howard Hughes was a spider caught in his own web. His true love was dwelling with his thoughts, enjoying nature, and building a better mousetrap. His father, a genius in his own right, developed the drill bit invention that made him a millionaire. At age eighteen Howard inherited his father's millions, and Howard's inventive skills turned him into the richest, most influential man in the United States (possibly the world). A billionaire in those days was a rare find.

Jealousy, scorn, and hate for Howard Hughes were unfounded, for no one got close enough to him to know his thoughts (and much of the time his whereabouts). His motto was: "Do as I say, not what I do." He took full responsibility for his actions. In fact, he found no need to discuss or retract his thoughts or decisions. He was satisfied with himself and his final decisions. His seclusion made him impossible to debate. However, under investigation by a U.S. congressional committee, he alone fought and won his case. His legal courtroom ability so outclassed the learned congressmen, he was touted for president.

He loved women to own, not to hold. His moviemaking empire was not to increase his fabulous wealth but to satisfy his ego and moviemaking hobby and owning beautiful women (women he could own, provide lavish domiciles for, and probably never see).

His purchase and operation of "the secret empire" (the Warm Springs Ranch) was his most amazing secret accomplishment. The success of this million-acre ranch and ranges (a good share of the state of Nevada) was accomplished by the coauthor, Jim Haworth, and Hughes's trusted aides.

Jim Haworth, the only living person to come forth with a graphic account of "living with" Howard Hughes and his other empire, gives his down-to-earth early experiences, ranching for Howard Hughes and himself. If Jim could have rescued Howard Hughes from his abductors, Hughes would be living today on his Warm Springs paradise.

After Howard Hughes's death, his cousin and coadministrator, William R. Lummis, managed to eliminate the empire's mafia control and with Haworth's assistance sold this vast property to the Church of Latter-Day Saints of Salt Lake City, Utah.

To this day Jim Haworth personally leases the Warm Springs Ranch from the LDS for his raising of range cattle and fine paint horses as well as providing a home for Clint Baxter's breed of Blackjackshales Morgan horses.

Howard Hughes, His Other Empire, and His Man

Prologue

Howard Hughes's Dreamworld

Howard Hughes. *(Wide World Photos)*

The wonders of nature, man, and the world—these were the often-rehearsed solitary thoughts of the middle-aged king of fame and fortune, famous aviator, womanizer, industrial, and political giant.

Although he lived all this, had access to the world powers, and was the richest man in the United States, he sought a sanctum to escape from public scrutiny to privately enjoy uninhibited nature.

On this day in June, alone, Howard Robard Hughes was carefully guiding his own converted Douglas bomber in a criss-cross fashion across the vast southeastern Nevada desert. The plane was his San Limbo, which gave him access to the wide-open spaces. It gave him exclusive right to survey his Nevada holdings and plan for additional ventures and challenges.

His whereabouts unknown, Howard Hughes often flew over his Nevada oasis paradise, the Warm Springs Ranch.

Dwight Whitney, a writer, once quoted Howard Hughes's life ambitions: "What I'm really interested in is science, nature and its manifestations, the earth and the minerals that come of it."

Even while flying over the "ranch" and the rest of Nevada, he had visions of finding the gold that had been abandoned in the mineral-rich Nevada mountains.

While in San Limbo Howard Hughes flew in wide circles over the Lake Mead, Nevada, area which also took him over his Tonopah gold mines area and the small hotel where he had privately married his second wife, Jean Peters. After they were married, Jean was never sure of Howard or where he was.

Below, in the Moapa Valley, Howard saw the Las Vegas to Saint George, Utah, highway. Just north a few miles he saw a hidden emerald oasis. He had, earlier this morning, flown over the Grand Canyon and into the canyon to see the sunrise. Now, he was seeing this beautiful wonder of nature nestled in the southern Nevada mountain ranges and desert. *This beautiful utopia must be there for me,* he mused. As soon as he returned to Las Vegas, he called his Houston lawyer, Dick Gray. The order was to find the ranch's owner and buy it.

The Hughes Warm Springs Ranch, as it is now called, was soon purchased from Jean Peters Taylor, executrix of the Taylor estate (not Jean Peters, Hughes's wife).

This became Howard Hughes's big secret, his Shangri-la, his San Limbo, his other empire, a million acres of ranch and range covering five counties of Nevada mountains, canyons, and desert.

This was the answer to Howard Hughes's dream, his escape to untainted air, pure water, and land. Here this "filthy rich," demanding, overbearing, fading specimen of a stalwart man could rest in quiet San Limbo.

The Secret Howard Hughes

> Howard Hughes's greatest invention was not the world's largest flying boat, or flush-riveting for planes, or Jane Russell's cantilevered bra. It was his secrecy machine.
> —Keats, *Howard Hughes.* 1972

Most of Howard Hughes's life was held in secret. Although he was rich and famous, he shied from public attention. In his later years, paranoia for his privacy and whereabouts was protected by armed guards outside his sealed bedroom. He became hopelessly drug addicted with the help of his aides. During his manic depression, he was captivated by his aides and was at their mercy, never to return to his beautiful paradise.

He not only hid himself; he hid business transactions and secret bribes for presidents. He went so far as to hide his aides and his detectives. He hid his bookkeeping and his memos. He secretly hired CIA agents to keep his government dealings secret. His buying of governments was not to take over but to make his calculated wants understood for his safety and for the safety of the United States.

Howard Hughes, to keep the ranch purchase secret, first deeded it to Mr. and Mrs. R. W. Webb, Hughes Tool Company executives, his agents. Howard Hughes's greatest secret was his million-acre expanse of ranch and ranges he had silently surveyed and enjoyed during his solo flights in his remodeled air force bomber. His empathy for animals and wildlife was his own secret. He did not survive to live in his beautiful other empire mansion or to enjoy his six thousand head of cattle or his two hundred head of horses or the ranch's abundant wildlife and its hidden gold.

The demise of Howard Hughes prevented his living out his life with his animals and other secrets of his private empire. His private addiction, codeine, made available by his aides and doctors, caused his final paranoia and his untimely death on April 5, 1976. Many say he was already dead, but not brain dead, when he was finally airlifted by his aides from Mexico to his birthplace, Houston, Texas.

A Character Portrait: Inside Howard Hughes and His Other Empire

It has been said, "To understand Howard Hughes is to know him." Howard Robard Hughes's character is a chronological portrait of his singular life.

Hughes was guided by the inherited spirit and characteristics of his father and mother. As a boy he, by himself, made his own motorbike with old parts and a borrowed car battery. He was a valuable piece of property with a hands-off sign. As a man, if he had a desire for someone or his possessions, he bought them at any cost, whether it be beautiful women or the king of Saudi Arabia, in the latter case not to be selfish, but because he had a better idea for the safety of the United States.

At his ultimate, pursued by intimidators, no one but his aides ever saw him. He successfully piloted his lifelong dream, the Hercules (Spruce Goose), then retired to his secured bedroom, where messages and notes were relayed to him by a courier next in command.

Controlled power was Hughes's solitary goal. He spent millions on whims, such as the movie business and women. He was generous with those who helped him. He used his easy wealth as creative instrument and worked night and day to make it work.

He was a gifted, peculiarly distinctive perfectionist with inventive analytical and engineering intelligence, yet not a scholar. He did not graduate from high school but attended Cal Tech in California for a short time, admitted by his father's influence. Howard was a workaholic, spending hours, days, and nights building and perfecting his inventions. He was a nature lover and thrilled at exploring her bounty.

Nothing pleased him more than solo-flying his own aircraft creations while planning and surveying his empire. His ultimate claim to fame was planning, engineering, building, and flying the biggest aircraft in the world—the Hercules. He detested it being called the Spruce Goose by those who said it was a pile of lumber that wouldn't fly.

During his soloing in his aircraft creations (his San Limbo, so called because when his executives were queried as to his whereabouts, they replied, "He's in San Limbo") he discovered his other empire, a million-acre Nevada desert empire with the beautiful Warm Springs oasis and mansion.

Some called Howard Hughes an eccentric genius. If this was in flattery, I agree. He was an inherited biophysical, biophysiological phenomenon, without a birth certificate. His aunt Annette Gano Lummis vouched for his legal identity. He married twice. He had no children.

He was the most bizarre, mysterious, trite, misunderstood person in the world. He was not a sit-down, feet-on-the desk businessman. His office was his brain operating from a telephone booth or his secluded bedroom. He carried very little money. On one occasion he borrowed a dime from an aide to make a business call. He was generous to a fault with faithful people. He hated communism and crime in and out of government. His political deals were legitimate payment for services rendered for the common good.

He was a Texan with the inherited lust for the most, the biggest, and the best. Even Texas was not big enough for this billionaire.

Howard Hughes despised and avoided income taxes, not by illegal means, but by his guarded secrecy from the IRS. However, he spent millions of his fortune in research, development, and building aircraft and war materials for the U.S. government. Rather than pay huge income taxes, he founded the nonprofit, now-famous Howard Hughes Medical Research Institute and gave it to the Hughes Aircraft Corporation with provision for them to pay him lease back money.

His fear of the Atomic Energy Commission's atomic energy tests in Nevada caused him to find a new hiding place away from Las Vegas and his eventual sighting and purchase of his other empire, forty-five miles northeast of Las Vegas.

Only his ranch superintendent, Jim Haworth, a couple of aides, and the Clark County clerk knew the vastness of the Howard Hughes hideaway from which he was spirited to Mexico, where he was drugged and died on his own airplane.

1
Early Story of Warm Springs Ranch

Jim Haworth's uncle John Ovard knew about the killing. John was sixty-five at the time. Uncle John's grandfather was Benjamin Dry, a brother of the villain Alexander Dry. They were two rowdy eastern Texas boys. Alex was worse than rowdy; he was a hellion.

In late 1870 Alexander Dry and two other outlaws held up a bank in Texas. Alex drew on the sheriff and was too fast for the sheriff's gun. He didn't wait for questions or the posse that was hot on his heels. He was long gone before he reached the Texas state border. Texas, enduring the problems of being readmitted to the Union, was not concerned with further chasing of Dry.

Alex had heard of places to hide in Nevada and that gold was there to be found. Other outlaws had reported hideouts in the Moapa Indian country of southeastern Nevada. They were fairly friendly Indians of the Paiute tribe.

Eleanor Lamb, in her stories of the Moapa, Nevada, valley wrote: "Few words have been spoken or written about the widespread, yet secluded cattle kingdom known as the Warm Springs Ranch. The other side of the Howard Hughes's empire; it is far more awesome and inconceivable than all the rest of his mighty domain."

Jim Haworth agrees; the story by his Uncle John, who lived on the Livingston (nearby Moapa), bears out Eleanor

Lamb's assessment of Jim's history of the Warm Springs Ranch.

Alexander Dry, while making his Texas escape, found it necessary to shoot another sheriff and his deputy. The desert sun and heat on his sunburned face, the loss of one horse, shot because of a busted leg, and Alex's own banged-up condition were telling on his mean disposition when in 1871 he arrived at the Muddy River near the current tiny town of Moapa, Nevada, about fifty-five miles northeast of the little settlement of Las Vegas.

After Alex's miserable ordeals with man and nature, he couldn't believe his eyes. He thought this was a mirage as he peered with bloodshot eyes into the Muddy River Valley. The lush meadows, palm trees, and tall green foliage standing in a twisted row assured him of the presence of water. By midafternoon he was in his newfound oasis in the Nevada desert. He found springs among the boulders and trees. Pheasants and quail scattered as he and his horse plodded through the wild meadow grass. The twisted row of brush he had seen from the mountains was arrow weeds.

Alexander Dry was not to be foolish. He knew other bandits and renegades took the same "hoot owl" trail to find this hiding place in this unforgiving Nevada desert wasteland. Small piles of rocks reminded him they did not all make it. He also knew of the marauding Paiutes.

Alex, carrying only his gun and his rope, cautiously moved toward the trees and tall green grassy patches in the rocks, where he noticed a dripping rock shelf. On closer inspection, he saw bubbling water coming onto and off the shelf. Below the shelf was a large bowl in a huge rock formation. He immediately shed his shoes, and to his amazement, the water was warm. The water felt so good on his tired, sore feet, he came out of the pool, stripped off his grimy clothes, and jumped in. Feeling like a human being again, he climbed up to the shelf and found a spring producing warm water.

His first thought after his warm springs bath was to water his parched horse. He unsaddled and stripped old Buck of his bridle and rope and turned him loose in the pool. Alex was probably the first to learn the good of warm water for swimming a lame horse. Buck first lolled warm water in his mouth, raised his head to check the territory, then slowly drank his fill.

The Warm Springs pool Alexander Dry discovered. The rock shelf was the scene for modern movies like *The Black Stallion*. The black horse jumped from the high rock shelf into the pool. *(Photo, 1993, by Clint Baxter)*

The Texas Visitor

The next day, Dry found some manageable rocks and planned building a cabin. He told himself this sanctum would be his hideaway home. One of his first visitors was a friendly Paiute Indian who had come to the ranch to harvest arrow weeds for his arrows. He showed Alex how to make a roof of arrow weeds and where the stream from the warm springs wound its way down to the river bed. The Mormons still call this the Muddy River, and the Indian, with gestures, warned Alex that the now-dry river would suddenly become filled by the devil and Alex must be careful.

For the last several days Alex had seen only cactus and blowing sand. The first day at Warm Springs, he squeezed cactus juice for himself and Buck, but that didn't go very far. Alex set about gathering some dried arrow weeds and built a small fire and cooked some beans with the warm spring's pure water. After preparing his meal of beans and whiskey to wash it down, he cut some wild desert grass and tethered Buck. Then, slouched on a rock, Alex enjoyed his meal and scanned the scenery. He actually drank more than he ate, since he hadn't time to hunt a rabbit or pheasant to go with the beans. He unrolled his blanket and propped himself on a slanted rock, then slept till awakened by a lonely mountain lion screaming on top of a nearby cliff.

All Alex's saddlebag held to eat was jerky and beans. Next morning he pulled his hunting gun from its scabbard and searched the tall weeds and grass for whatever was to be found. He raised a pheasant, shot and plucked it, found its nest, and for a late breakfast had pheasant and eggs with his jerky. He had no coffee but made do with hot water and fresh mint from a wet area near the spring.

After breakfast, he concentrated on his plan for a cabin. He spent the next two days gathering rocks. The one-room rock hut with an arrow weed roof was completed after two weeks of backbreaking work in the hot sun. He did take breaks to jump in his pool, relax, and look at his handiwork and enjoy his oasis in the green Warm Spring Valley. He called his home Stone Cabin Springs.

Alex Dry rustled a few head of cattle and horses and settled down to a new life of ranching and enjoying his rugged solo life away from bounty hunters and poachers.

Alexander Dry enjoyed his solitary life, running horses and cattle, but in 1876, after only two years of lonely bliss, he was surprised by a renegade outlaw. Alex didn't recognize the ragged poor excuse for a man as his laden mule carried him across the shimmering sand. He turned out to be wanted for a Texas holdup and murder. After a few days of drinking and quarreling about possible gold under Alex's cabin, the bandit, John Hanley, challenged Alex. Alex Dry shot Hanley off his mule. Dry, with no remorse or guilt, buried Hanley behind his cabin.

Dry continued to run his horses and cattle in the valley and nearby ranges while renegades and horse thieves were seeking him out. One day in 1882, Dry came upon an outlaw named Jack Longstreet branding one of his calves. Without opportunity for fair gunplay, Longstreet swung his gun, and when the smoke cleared, Alexander Dry lay dead on the ground. Later Dry was found. The bullet was in the back of his head, and his gun was jammed.

During the late 1870's and early '80s, many outlaws and prospectors searched the area for gold. None was found and the ranch lay idle until 1889, being taken over by the Paiute Indians.

The Mormons settled the valley town of Overton in 1870. They were soon driven out by malaria and smallpox. All the inhabitants of the valley were sick. Most everyone pulled out,

A Jim Haworth drawing of the Alexander Dry–John Hanley incident.

except the Indians and the outlaws who stayed on Warm Springs Ranch.

Also at that time, the Mormons Dudley Leavitt and Edward Bunker were settling the Virgin River area (thirty miles away).

One of the Mormon pioneers moved onto the Warm Springs homestead in 1889 and set up ranching. This Mormon pioneer was Bill Liston. He cleared the mesquite and raised some alfalfa, tobacco, and cotton on about thirty acres of the land.

Meanwhile, during the time of Liston's occupation of the ranch, Howard Hughes was born in Houston, Texas, on

Christmas Eve, 1905. In 1909, Howard Hughes's father invented the Hughes rock bit (the roller bit for oil well drilling).[1]

Calvin Beach acquired the Home Ranch, as it was then called, in 1912. (In 1912, Walter D. Sharp, partner in Hughes-Sharpe (sic) Tool Company, died.) Calvin Beach and his brother-in-law, a man named Fitzgerald, ran cattle a few years and built most of the present ranch buildings. Also, George Baldwin (for whom the present Baldwin Springs is named) ran cattle on leased land at the upper end of the ranch for a short time in 1918. He liked to gamble over at the Las Vegas Club, playing with Cal Housel, the owner, till he lost his ass—Cal had racehorses and several stables and a training track (path). Cal Housel gave Baldwin a new pickup and seventy-five dollars a month the rest of his life, and Baldwin took off to enjoy himself. A man named Buffington from Wyoming then leased the Home Ranch before Fitzgerald leased the ranch for a second time from 1919 to 1923.

From 1923 until 1929, U. V. Perkins leased the Home Ranch. (In 1923 Howard Hughes went to Cal Tech, Pasadena, without a high school diploma.)

In 1928, Hughes signed over his Houston homestead to Aunt Annette, Fred R. Lummis, and family.

During the Prohibition days of the twenties, a considerable amount of moonshine was made along the Big Muddy River in this Moapa Valley. Of course, the Paiute Indians made use of it. In 1920, a man named McKay had whiskey stills hidden in several places on the ranch. The warm water was ideal for the purpose. Carloads of sugar coming into Moapa alerted the federal authorities, and McKay went to federal prison.

In 1930 Howard Hughes purchased 7000 Romaine Street, Los Angeles, for movie making and girl buying. During 1930 and 1931 a Mr. Francisco was caretaker of the Home Ranch. In 1932 Howard Hughes started racing airplanes and motorcycles and acquiring more women and movies, all under the Hughes Tool Company name. In 1932 Clayton "Droopy" Phillips bought the ranch from Calvin Beach. When Phillips was not able to make the payments, the ranch returned to Cal Beach. Cal Beach died leaving the ranch to his former partner, Fitzgerald. Fitzgerald died leaving the ranch to his daughters, Mrs. Mary Hawkins and Mrs. Ray Weber.

Jim Haworth drawing of headquarters, Warm Springs Ranch.

The Thirties

In 1927 Howard Hughes made 7000 Romaine Street, in Los Angeles, his moviemaking headquarters. He was busy filming *Hell's Angels*. He especially enjoyed the aerial combat sequences. He bought and leased seventy World War I fighting planes, giving him the largest private air force in the world, at a cost of over half a million dollars. He hired war heroes to fly them. Three of his men died in the filming, and he crashed his rotary-powered Morse, which he had never flown before. His facial injuries left permanent scars, probably accounting for his later growing a mustache, and added to his seclusion from scrutiny.

Howard Hughes moved the aerial scenes to San Francisco, leaving his wife, Ella, at home. She walked out on him. Although she loved him, she could no longer play second fiddle to his obsessive moviemaking.

After Ella left, Howard signed over the family home in Houston to his favorite aunt, Annette Gano, who had raised him after his mother died. Annette Gano and her friend Estelle Sharp were those who signed an affidavit as proof of when and where Howard was born. He had no birth certificate.

At the age of sixteen Howard received word of his mother, Allene Hughes's death. Aunt Annette was mother to him thereafter. Howard Hughes's favorite cousin, William R. Lummis, Annette's son, was later to become coadministrator of Howard Hughes's estate.

After a few years of Aunt Annette's careful custody, Howard gave her the family home without a deed in Houston. After giving the family home to Aunt Annette, Howard realized he was more sentimentally attached to the family home than was Aunt Annette, and excluded Aunt Annette and all the rest of his mother's relatives from his will. He had earlier, in 1925, excluded all his father's relatives from his life.

Howard and Ella were divorced on December 9, 1929.

Howard Hughes decided to refilm *Hell's Angels* with some spice. He hired Jean Harlow for her sexual appeal. She had the enticing, naturally high, firm breasts and the build and blond hair that assured him she was right for the part. That was the real beginning of blatantly sexual movies in Hollywood. He hired Jean Harlow for six weeks for $1,500, completed *Hell's Angels* in 1930, then sold her contract to MGM for $60,000, a lot of money in the Great Depression.

Hughes claimed the *Hell's Angels* movie was for publicity purposes and boasted a $2 million profit, while his financial adviser, Noah Dietrick, said it was a $1.5 million loss. Dietrick's advice was a lesson for Howard—never disclose his profits. That was OK for Howard, since he had never paid federal income tax up to this point in time. The *Hell's Angels* film made Hughes, now twenty-six years old, a plum for the most eligible Hollywood actresses. Even the most popular of Hollywood were seeking his employment.

Notes

1. Howard Hughes's father invented the first roller bit to crack through solid rock in search for oil.

2

The Early Life and Trials of James S. Haworth

Born in Ogden, Utah, November 26, 1918, Jim Haworth was orphaned at six years of age. Uncle John Ovard took him to Moapa, Nevada, the Livingston Ranch. Ever since he has lived on or near the Warm Springs Ranch in southern Nevada.

Jim graduated from Moapa Valley High School in the year of 1939. The Moapa Valley High School consisted of 100 pupils and six teachers for the four years of high school. His interest was in girls, horses, physical education classes, and seeing Iris, his future wife. In his spare time he wrangled cattle and rode the range.

Jim married Iris Lena Leavitt on June 23, 1939, in Kingman, Arizona—too young to get a license in Nevada.

Jim worked around the Moapa Valley for about a year until he starved out. He went to Nelson, Nevada, to work in the mines, but not for long. His feet wouldn't stay still down there in that dark hole, so he and Iris leased the Home Ranch, now known as the Hughes Warm Springs Ranch, and started raising horses and cattle, which they did until 1942, when Mr. Griffith, owner of the Last Frontier Hotel, bought the ranch and bought out their lease for $10,000 plus livestock for $5,000.

Before they leased the Home Ranch, Iris and Jim used to camp over across the creek. They were just a couple of kids.

Jim Haworth.

Jim Haworth and his wife, Iris Lena Leavitt.

There they saw two outlaws, Ed and Bill Gannel, who supplied them with beef although they had no cattle.

During the first three years after they were married, Iris had two boys; the first boy died in a couple of days. Then their son, Jerry, was born in 1942. He now has a family of his own and lives in Logandale, near Moapa.

The Haworths moved from the Home Ranch to Coos Bay, Oregon, then came back to Fallon, Nevada, and bought a small ranch. They lived there until the armed service put Jim in the navy. (Imagine a cowpuncher in the navy!)

Jim was mustered out in 1944 after about six months. The war had ended.

Then the Haworths sold their place in Fallon, Nevada, and moved to Las Vegas and bought a new home.

Their daughter, Rita Jane, was born in 1944 in Las Vegas.

For about two years, Jim and Iris went in as partners with L. R. Ivans in the dairy business in the Moapa Valley, where they bought a small ranch, selling their Las Vegas home. After a couple of years of starvation, they sold out again and Jim went to work in construction until they finally got the wrinkles out of their stomachs. He didn't know it at the time, but he got some valuable experience in ranch management and treatment of cattle, later put to good use with Mr. Hughes's ranch.

In 1952, Jim went to work for Frank Taylor, a millionaire from New York who had bought the Home Ranch and built a mansion for his wife. Jim worked there for a while, becoming his ranch manager and doing something he liked. He became a cattle partner with Mr. Taylor and stayed on for sixteen years, until Mr. Taylor died.

While Jim was working for Frank (Francis) Taylor, Iris and he bought range rights and a herd of cattle in Lincoln County from Mr. Taylor. They picked up property any time they got a chance and have been selling some of it off as needed.

In 1968, when Mr. Taylor died, Howard R. Hughes bought the ranch and Jim stayed on as manager for Mr. Hughes for ten more years,[1] 26 years in all on the Warm Springs Ranch, now called the Hughes Warms Springs Ranch.

Mr. Hughes let Jim build up the ranch empire to a little over a million acres, counting the BLM range land, and at one time they had six thousand head of cattle, which was quite an operation for Jim, but he enjoyed every minute working for two great men like Frank Taylor and Howard Hughes. Jim got to do a lot of traveling, showing cattle and horses. He spent evenings learning to draw pictures of what he had seen during the days. He met Howard Hughes's executives socially and on business.

Jim met a great many interesting people. He stayed with Howard Hughes until he died in 1976; then the company sold out to the LDS church. Jim managed the ranch operation for the church for five years. That was quite interesting, working for about twenty LDS bosses.

After five years, Jim couldn't fight the battle any longer, so he resigned, a total wreck, and retired for a couple of years, but retirement wasn't for him.

He then leased 1,200 acres of the Warm Springs Ranch from the church and is back to raising cattle and horses in the fabulous Hughes's other empire that he only saw from the sky. He has about as good a herd of paint horses as anyone can raise. He boards and cares for Clint Baxter's beautiful black Morgan horses.

Jim and Iris's daughter, Rita, born in 1944, has two grown sons. She works for the Logandale School District. One boy, Jimmy, works for the Cal Nevada Pipe Line Company, and the other, Todd, works at the Metro Police Department in Las Vegas. Jim and Iris have six grandchildren and two great-granddaughters and have really enjoyed them. So all in all,

Jim has had a very exciting and enjoyable life, especially during his years on the Howard Hughes Warm Springs Ranch.

Jim and Iris's son, Jerry lives and works in Logandale. He works for Nevada Power in Moapa and has a son, Travis, who has three daughters; Melissa, Jenniffer, and Brittney. Jim's son and grandsons help on the ranch when they can.

The Warm Springs Ranch as I Saw It, by Iris Haworth

Our beginning on the Warm Springs Ranch was in the early forties. It was then called the Home Ranch.

The ranch had been vacant for about fifteen years. The grass had grown high, the bushes were thick, and the tall palm trees with their skirts hanging to the ground were, in places, like rooms. The large cottonwood and ash trees spread their branches across the lane that was the entrance into the ranch, where three old homes were set back in the palm trees.

After Jim quit work in the mines, we moved to the Home Ranch. Jim and I rode our horses through the ranch and decided that we could really increase our horses and cows if we leased it, because the pastures were beautiful, with plenty of grass. We got in touch with the two sisters, Mrs. Hawkins and Mrs. Weber, who had inherited it from their father. In only a short time we had our lease and were ready to move up.

In May 1941, we put our furniture and other household belongings in our pickup and Jim gathered his horses and cattle from the Livingston Ranch, which is now the Hidden Valley Ranch.

When I got to the Home Ranch, Jim was still driving livestock up through the Moapa Indian reservation and hills.

The day had been long, and I arrived at the ranch a little after dark. As I turned in the lane it was so silent, at first I could not see a light at all, as our only neighbor was across a large field, with a lot of trees and shrubs between.

There was no power, and our few neighbors used coal oil lamps.

I heard a terrible noise like a scream. I stopped the truck and there was another louder scream.

I froze and put my pickup in reverse and started backing up and turned around. I never stopped until I got away from the ranch and on top of the hill called Battleship. I knew Jim would have to go right by me. In about thirty minutes I could hear him coming. When he got to me he was concerned about me, waiting in the pickup, and I told him that some awful screaming was at the ranch. He told me that it was the wild peacocks, and, of course, I then remembered seeing them but hadn't really heard them. Later I appreciated having them for their beauty, and they are very good watchdogs. They yelled every time someone entered the ranch. Also, one old guinea hen ran around as if she owned the place.

The first thing Jim and I started to do was fix and clean our house. We then moved in what at the time was the cook house. This house had been used to feed all the help.

We painted, hung wallpaper, and, most important, had electric power put in. After new linoleum had been laid, things looked pretty good and Jim hired a young man called Jeff to help with all the farming and an elderly man who cut wood to keep the wood cook stove going, along with doing other chores such as feeding and caring for the animals.

We had a nice warm spring that ran into a small swimming pool, and there was a dressing room. We bathed there every day, and in the summer we used it several times a day to relax a little.

The work was long and hard. Jim and I took care of the livestock and worked the ranch. Everyone kept busy and the place started to shape up.

We took in cattle and horses to board in the pasture and both took time riding the pasture to take count.

In the fall we put up a lot of corn for our hogs, which had increased to about ninety head, and plenty of hay for cattle.

We did have a lot of company. Our friends started coming and stayed overnight. Many came that had never seen the ranch. It looked like a desert oasis all alone in the desert.

Friends started coming, wanting to ride and help with the branding and other work, and in the evening we could swim and even had dances with a record player.

Then a retired couple who owned the lease above us rented the house next to us on the ranch and I had a lady friend there, which made me feel better, as I was pregnant and Jim and I were nervous. We called our family doctor, who had to come about twenty-five miles. He always came and we became good friends. In December 1942, our son, Jerry, arrived, a healthy, happy baby, and of course everyone wanted to take him and he got a lot of attention.

The place really started shaping up, and with the grass cut, flowers planted and blooming, more people started coming and then Mr. Griffith, the owner of the Last Frontier Hotel, came over and looked at the place and, of course, he wanted it. He bought the Home Ranch and our lease from the two Fitzgerald sisters. He also bought the Livingston Ranch.

He bought our leased livestock, and we decided to stay and manage the ranches until they got started.

Then they decided to put Jim as manager at the Livingston Ranch and we moved back in our old home there, but it was not the same for me and we had money to start on a ranch of our own. But first the family doctor wanted us to go to Coos Bay, Oregon, to manage his ranch. After two weeks the Oregon rain was too much for us.

So we decided to come back to Nevada near our friends who had bought a ranch at Fallon, and as we came back through to see them we found a ranch nearby, which we bought, doing everything that goes with ranching.

World War II was going on, so Jim enlisted in the navy. We sold our Fallon ranch and came back to Las Vegas in southern Nevada. We bought a home in Las Vegas and I stayed there with our son, Jerry, while Jim was in the navy.

The war ended and Jim came home. Our daughter, Rita Jane, was born in 1944.

Then we were partners with L. R. Ivans in a small dairy business and bought a small ranch in Moapa Valley. We sold out in about two years.

During this time the Frontier Hotel owned the Home Ranch. A rich man named Frank Taylor, from the East, came west and liked the ranch, and soon he became the owner.

Jim and I met the new owner, and soon Jim was helping him buy cattle from different parts of the United States. They were hauled in his large semi truck.

Time went by and Jim was quickly buying more ranches and ranges for Frank Taylor. Jim also bought cattle and horses for himself.

The ranges spread from Gold Butte to Caliente.

We soon moved back into our old house on the ranch. As manager this time, Jim started working the ranch and riding the vast ranges with the cowboys.

There were not many dull moments, but we would have our breaks with large barbecues, sometimes music. Lots of people were invited to join in the fun.

Our family was there for sixteen years. When Frank Taylor passed away, his widow soon sold to Mr. Hughes. Jim helped Mr Hughes buy more ranches until Jim managed about a million acres for Mr. Howard Hughes and it became known as the Hughes Warm Springs Ranch.

Notes

1. Howard Hughes died in 1976, but Jim Haworth continued working for the ranch until the estate was settled soon after. Then Jim Haworth stayed on as manager of the Warm Springs Ranch for the LDS Church for another five years. The LDS Church abandoned their use of the Warm Springs Ranch and Jim and Iris then leased the ranch from the LDS Church. They are to this day running the ranch and raising paint horses and cattle.

3

Howard Hughes's Younger Years

A light shuffling of the gravel outside the open door attracted their attention.

"Who is that skinny rat of a kid?" yelled a voice from the station. A startled three-year-old local waif had appeared at the open door of Station 8 of the Houston Fire Department. Another of the firemen spoke up: "Why, that's Mrs. Hughes's fancy kid. She handles him with kid gloves while his dad is playing around with oil wells, gettin' rich."

The foursome were seated at their daily afternoon pinochle card game. Henry, the dealer, stopped short of completing his chore to motion the shy, reluctant neophyte into the station's dome of silence, where the only interruptions were an occasional fire call or a call for a cat in a tree. Henry left the table, pulled up a stool and said, "Sit there and be quiet. I want to talk to you. What's your name?"

Without hesitation, the polite little fellow stated proudly, though shaken by the fireman's unwelcome shout, "I am Howard Robard Hughes. My daddy is an oilman, and my mother will be looking in our yard for me over there."

Howard Robard Hughes was born Christmas Eve, 1905, to Howard Robard Hughes, Sr., and Allene Hughes in their small house in a modest neighborhood at 1402 Crawford Street in Houston, Texas, where his father practiced law, studied his oil well investments, and spent money around the southwest like a trooper. The elder Hugheses had married four years earlier, after a lucrative year of Robert Hughes's oil investments. In that year he purchased and sold oil properties that yielded a profit of $50,000, which he immediately spent on their lavish wedding trip to Europe.

Howard Senior, as he was called, had the knack for making money, and he spent it in a fashion only believed by those who knew him.

When Howard (called Sonny by his dad) was born that blustery Christmas Eve, his dad was too involved attending to his legal and financial skills to register a birth certificate for Howard. Later, Howard's aunt, Annette Gano, vouched for having seen him born. Aunt Annette and Sonny's mother raised and protected him while his dad traveled, invested, and worked oil wells in several of the southwestern states, meanwhile dressing splendidly and entertaining the social elite. He was away from home so often he felt most comfortable living in lavish hotel suites and socializing with the movie set.

Howard inherited from his father the urge to secretly explore and enjoy nature.

Mrs. Hughes instilled Howard's phobias pertaining to his physical and mental well-being. The dreaded dangers of microbial diseases and isolation from his peers, his inherent fear for safe health, and his isolationism preyed on Howard's mind and fashioned his entire life. Probably his first introduction to the outside world that day at the firehouse was cause for his change of character as a child who was seen and not heard to one heard and not seen. His interest in engineering started on that day. Many questions about fire engines were fielded and answered before the battalion chief took Sonny home.

Howard was close to his mother in a formal way. He was not one to rush up, throw his arms around her and kiss her. At her urging, he kissed her lightly on the cheek. All this plus his deafness had much to do with his permanent psychophysical condition, causing him to live like a clam, leading later to his self-destruction.

Howard's deafness was his inherited disability.

Howard's mother observed his early interest (even as a three-year-old) in mechanical equipment of all sorts, while Hughes Senior was engrossed in tinkering in his shop. Dad was always thinking of some oil well improvement. While scratching out drawings for his oil well drills he came upon the idea of the Hughes roller bit, which would penetrate through dense rock strata, heretofore never successfully attained. The geologists of the time were fairly sure huge oil reserves lay under those hard subsurface rock formations. This oil well drill bit was the source of the Hughes family's fabulous fortune, from which Howard Hughes, Jr., became a billionaire.

When Howard (Sonny) was a teenager his mother was still worried about his health, especially when he visited his uncles. She worried about his feet, his teeth, his digestion, and his elimination. This caused Howard to feign illness to get attention. When Howard was thirteen, fear of the infantile paralysis epidemic nearly did his mother in. She placed Sonny in isolation. This plus his inherited hearing problem added to his antisocial behavior.

Howard Senior's plans for his oil well roller drill bit with 166 cutting edges were drawn on a breadboard on his wife's dining room table. Fearful of being victimized, he hurried with the plans to a Massachusetts tool shop for manufacture of a pilot model. He was cunning with his thoughts and secrets and secretive with his findings, as was Howard Hughes, Jr., in later years. The roller bit was soon patented, and with his partner, Walter D. Sharp, Howard Senior formed the Hughes-Sharpe Tool Company. The bits were not for sale but were leased at $30,000 per well, whether the well was productive or not, and then re-leased to the next customer.

As Sonny grew, his principal interest remained mechanical toys and how they worked. Sonny was a loner. He occasionally played with his father's partner's little boy, Dudley Sharp, but usually Sonny could be found in his room, which reeked of oil, or in a little shop behind the house. His father provided tools for him to play with.

By the time Sonny was ten he was inventing mechanical items in his shop, all for his own pleasure. He invented his own ham radio set while his dreams of speed were budding. He invented his own motorbike by converting his bicycle to one powered by a storage battery complete with a self-starter motor taken from his father's automobile.

At fourteen, Sonny, with his father, attended a Harvard versus Yale crew race. This was Howard's first introduction to the wonders of nature and man. While there, he saw a seaplane majestically take to the air like a Canada goose. Then and there he decided he was going to fly, His father reluctantly took Howard on a ten-dollar ride in the seaplane. This was the impetus for Howard's lifelong love of aircraft and speed and his eventual building the world's largest aircraft, the Hercules (Spruce Goose).

Howard's father's life was now the light fantastic with the rapid wealth from his drill bit invention. He threw social parties, provided Sonny's mother with elegant clothes and furs, and maintained a yacht. His tool company had grown so fast executives were hired to run it for him. After a long illness, his partner died November 28, 1912. Howard Hughes, Sr., bought Sharp's half of the company from Sharp's widow, and then it became Hughes Tool Company.

At sixteen, in 1921, Howard graduated from Fessenden School in Boston (this was at an eighth-grade level). During his time at Fessenden he bought and rode a horse for his solitary pleasure. This was the start of Howard's natural love for animals, later, to lead to his purchase of a million-acre

Nevada ranch (the Warm Springs Ranch) and range for thousands of cattle and horses.

Howard's father then sent him to Ojai, California, to Thatcher College, while he opened a tool company branch in Los Angeles.

Howard Hughes, Sr., had an interrupted education, which seemed to have been inherited by Sonny. When Howard Senior was a young man of seventeen, he left Iowa State Law School, passed the bar, and went to work for his father in his father's law practice in Houston.

In 1923, at eighteen, Howard Hughes, Jr. left Thatcher and his father pulled strings to enroll him in Cal Tech Pasadena without a high school diploma. He was a poor student except for his tutored geometry. He was an excellent scholar in subjects of his interest. In those, he excelled as a genius.

During this time, Uncle Rupert Hughes cut quite a swath in Hollywood. Uncle Rupert talked Sam Goldwyn away from acting and into switching to making silent movies and Rupert earned as much as $125,000 per year. In 1921, Mother Hughes died and Sonny "existed" on his father's wealth. His father took him to the gambling ladies' world of tinsel, evening clothes, Prohibition, and whiskey—a "finishing school" for Sonny, the introvert. All this wealth allowed Sonny to seek his own pleasures—racing cars, flight lessons, golf, and so forth. He took flying lessons from several instructors, and cross-matched their knowledge with his, spending hours discussing the function of the critical parts of the aircraft.

Hughes Tool Company rapidly expanded to a worth of $70 million to $80 million and Sonny received a $5,000 a month allowance.

Sonny attended Rice Institute for a semester but wanted to leave Houston, and strike out on his own. After his father died in January 1924, Sonny became Howard Hughes, the three-quarter owner of Hughes Tool Company, and at eighteen he changed his wanderlust mind to aggressively claim his inheritance. Howard inherited through his father's will one-fourth of the estate and all his departed mother's half of the estate. The one-fourth remaining was left to the older Hughes brother and Howard's grandfather and grandmother. This was quickly purchased by Howard after he gained control of the Howard Hughes (Hughes Tool) Company.

His uncle, his father's brother Felix, wanted to become Howard's guardian. Howard saw the probability that the Hughes Tool Company would be out of his control if this took place. He appealed for himself at the estate hearings to prove he was capable of handling the estate while his aunts and uncles claimed he could not until he was twenty-one. Through many hearings the determined Howard represented himself and was able to convince the judge that he was capable at eighteen to inherit and run the Hughes Tool Company.

His next move was the successful purchase of the remaining 25 percent of the Hughes Tool Company from his relatives.

After Howard became complete owner of Hughes Tool Company, Mrs. Walter Sharp took him and his friend Dudley to Europe, where Sonny became fascinated with casino play. With a $10 plaque he built up his red and black winnings to $10,000. He placed a final wager of $10, lost it, and left with $9,990. This completed his venture into gambling. He'd rather own the place.

On the steamer home, he and Dudley were ushered to a first-class but small cabin. Sonny, very much the wealthy entrepreneur, insisting he be called Mr. Howard Hughes, went directly to the captain and demanded the largest, best, and most expensive cabin on the ship. This was the first of Howard's adventures in "money talking." He could buy anything and influence anyone he wanted.

Aunt Annette married a Rice relative, Dr. Fred Lummis. (William R. Lummis, their son, and Howard's cousin, later became coadministrator of Hughes's estate [Summa Corporation] after Hughes's death.)

Howard Hughes now had the vision of investing and building his father's millions into his own billions.

Later some of his investments might seem like playthings, but Howard worked very hard to make them succeed under his sole control. He spent millions with one purpose: to succeed.

Embarking on a Career with a Bride

Now, at age twenty, there were new worlds for conquest. With full control of Hughes Tool Company, like his father, Howard seldom went to the plant, as he did not want to meddle with his fertile nest egg. This approach to an inherited fortune was soon dismissed, as he became personally involved in control of each of his whims and empire dreams.

Meanwhile, he became reacquainted with Ella Rice, a girl he had met as a youngster at a Christ Church Cathedral social where she was crowned queen. Ella Rice was the great-grandniece of the founder of Rice Institute. Now, though rich, Howard did not appeal to the young ladies. He often attended social events, but alone.

With Ella, it was a one-sided love. She paid little attention to this boy, two years younger than she. He did manage to date her several times and asked her to marry him. When she refused, Howard turned to Aunt Annette for help. As always, he could depend on her influence when needed. After all, Annette, also a member of the Rice family, was now married to Frederick R. Lummis, a noted Texas lawyer. Aunt Annette was a grand-niece of Rice Institute founder William Marsh

Rice. Aunt Annette Gano Lummis convinced her mother, Great-aunt Mattie, to let Ella marry Howard so he would not go to California alone with all that money. Ella agreed, and the wedding was scheduled and held June 1, 1925.

Instead of socializing, and attending bachelor parties, Howard worried about impostors and spent laborious days writing his will. The will was voluminous, but his wishes were quite specific:

- To his friend, Dudley C. Sharp, $10,000
- To his uncle, Chilton Gano, $15,000
- To his aunt Mrs. Thomas P. Hustoun, $25,000
- To his aunt Annette (Mrs. Fred R. Lummis) $100,000 and his home on Yoakum Boulevard
- To his wife, Ella Rice Hughes, $500,000 in high-grade securities, to be delivered as soon as possible after his death
- To Lily Adams and John Farrell (black household servants), a weekly pension of $20 each
- To six executives of Hughes Tool Company, 1 percent to 5 percent of the company's dividends

Conspicuously absent from nineteen-year-old Howard Hughes's will was any bequest to Uncle Rupert, Uncle Felix, grandparents Felix and Jean Hughes, or any other relative on his father's side.

Remaining assets were to establish and build the Howard R. Hughes Medical Research Laboratory (not a hospital) headed by a three-man board of trustees: Frank Andrews, tool company lawyer; Dr. Fred R. Lummis, Annette's husband; and Frederick C. Prottor, family friend. These three were also to be the estate's executors.

Also, Howard's father's tool company would be preserved. Howard worked for weeks on the will with Frank

Andrews, once his father's lawyer and now his. The will was signed May 10, 1925.

Howard worked that summer on his steam-powered car and played golf, then took his bride to Dallas to show his cousins and was ready to move to California. He had Aunt Annette talked into moving to California also. He and Ella took a private train coach to Hollywood. He needed to prove himself, and Hollywood was just the dreamworld for him. There was lots of adventure and excitement waiting for him. He realized no need for a profit motive. However, his dream of successful control of his destiny was uppermost in his mind.

Howard and Ella, Houston to Hollywood

Howard Hughes and Ella Rice Hughes had an uneventful but exciting trip in their private sleeper on that 1925 train to California. The excitement was not the train ride, but the anticipation of involvement in the glamour of Hollywood.

Their first residence was one of the luxury cottages in the beautiful gardens surrounding an Olympic-size pool of the ornate Ambassador Hotel on Wilshire Boulevard, the same hotel at which Howard's father had so lavishly entertained movie celebrities.

Uncle Rupert had already established residence in Hollywood and was earning $250,000 a year in his movie business. Howard used to occasionally visit Uncle Rupert, but these were unhappy occasions for Howard. Uncle Rupert was busy with the Goldwyn Studios, with little time for Howard.

Howard was soon involved in movie-making. His first venture was with Ralph Graves, a former Hughes Tool Company employee. They acquired the story called "Swell Hogan." Although Howard invested $60,000, and worked hard, the movie was a flop, never released.

The Hughes family, especially Uncle Rupert, was afraid Howard would squander his inheritance, thereby ruining his relatives. However, Howard was more determined than ever to produce movies. He considered his first movie a learning experience, not a waste. He quickly contacted a family friend, Marshall Neilon, and they produced *Everybody's Acting* and made a small profit.

Howard and Ella left the Ambassador Hotel and moved into a luxurious home new with a back entrance to the elite Wilshire Country Club Golf Course. This satisfied Howard's frequent urge to play his favorite game. His satisfaction with beautiful women was knowing he owned the best for his movies.

His next project was establishment of his own movie studio. He amended the charter of a Hughes Tool Company rock bit subsidiary called Caddo Rock Drill Bit Company of Louisiana to Caddo's of Hollywood. Next, he placed Noah Dietrick as supervisor of Caddo's of Hollywood. Dietrick had, since 1925, worked for Howard as a certified public accountant in Houston. Noah Dietrick became Hughes's financial adviser and was given charge of all investments.

Howard Hughes was fortunate in obtaining (for Caddo) Lewis Milestone, after he left Warner Brothers, as his director for a successful movie called *Two Arabian Knights*, at a cost of $500,000. Howard was now a big-time movie producer. He was a socializer for his first and last time. His appearances in the public eye were either alone at social gatherings or with several famous actresses. Scant time was spent with Ella. In October 1928, she left their home and returned to Houston. Almost immediately the incensed Howard signed over to Aunt Annette Lummis his Houston home on Yoakum Boulevard, where she had been living with her husband, Frederick R. Lummis, and family. This was probably the most important event in the later litigation into Howard Hughes's will.

Howard Hughes wanted Annette Lummis, Fred Lummis, and family to remain in Howard's father's home, for it was his lone sentimental inheritance from Howard Hughes, Sr.

Aunt Annette wanted to move to a larger home. Howard pleaded with her, promising a beautiful addition to the home and grounds. Annette finally agreed to remain in the house with her family. Soon, within a few months, Howard rewrote his will excluding Annette and all her relatives. He had formerly excluded all his father's family from his will. Since Ella's leaving him alone in Hollywood, she was also excluded from the will. Howard wanted the bulk of his estate to go to his charity, The Howard Hughes Medical Research Foundation, his legitimate dodge from income taxes.

In December 1929, Howard and Ella were divorced. The will was never found.

An interesting analysis of Howard's shrewd financial manipulations to save on income tax and continue his spending spree was his establishment of the Research Charitable Institute by Hughes Tool Company (his tool company) as a charitable tax deduction. This left the otherwise tremendous tax burden (never proven) for the billionaire's investments in aircraft, electronics, war materials and other necessary expenditures for the air force. He invested in war contracts to satisfy his ego, plus profit. His "investments" in movie-making and actresses were for pleasure and profit. He always loved movies. He loved his collection of beautiful women, to hold, but not too close.

He went ahead with, what would be his best movie, *Hell's Angels,* staring Jean Harlow (at $1,500 for the entire contract). Later he sold Jean Harlow to MGM for $60,000. In spite of *Hell's Angels'* successful showing, according to Noah Dietrick it did not make its production costs of $3.8 million.

In 1932 Howard renewed his lifelong interest—building (remodeling) his own airplane for racing. It was an air force plane built by Boeing as a military pursuit plane, not for private use. By governmental "arrangements," Howard had the distinct privilege of being the only private citizen to own one.

He leased a small area of Lockheed Aircraft Corporation in Burbank for his shop. The hobby project grew with a larger building and many employees. It became Hughes Aircraft Company, later to become one of America's largest and most powerful defense contractors. Howard's flying "hobby" was no longer a hobby, it caused IRS concern for taxes. Howard had anticipated this and kept all files carefully guarded and secret.

Howard studied flying and, to gain additional experience, worked for American Airways. He flew one time from Los Angeles to New York under the name of Charles W. Howard. Then he resigned, never to work for another again.

He entered his plane in a Miami race in 1934. His plane had a 580 HP Wasp engine and traveled easily at 335 miles per hour. He won the 20-hour race at an average of 185.7 miles per hour.

While traveling to Miami, Howard stopped in Houston to visit Aunt Annette Lummis in his home. He visited with Annette's two sons and two daughters. He was especially taken with Annette's oldest son, William Rice Lummis (Willie), then four years old. In a rare letter written later to Annette, Howard expressed his favor for Willie as an *adorable* child.

Winning the Miami race stimulated Howard's thinking of a plan for a faster plane. He could have easily hired an airplane designer and manufacturer to do the job, but, true to Howard's inherited character, he decided to design and build it himself. He hired a team of new graduates from Cal Tech.

A job, any job, during that time of depression, especially working for Howard Hughes, was an opportunity not to miss. These eager young men under supervisor Glenn Odekirk (himself a competent pilot and mechanic) went to work building a plane for Hughes that could fly faster and higher than any other in the world. The wooden miniature models were tested in Cal Tech's wind tunnel.

Howard Hughes, known as the true-life "Tom Swift," took his men and model to the Grand Central Airport in Glendale, California, walled off a leased section, and went to work building his mystery plane, named *H-1* by the crew.

Howard Hughes, the thinker, knew now how to get technical answers and with them fashioned his own inventions. Credit was given him for his amazing engineering and inventive accomplishments, although others provided him the tools to build them.

The Hughes Tool Company Houston employees were now praising Howard's aircraft accomplishments, while his president and general manager, Col. R. C. Kuldell, wished Howard had stayed with movie-making. He was afraid Howard would kill himself in an airplane, with no will. The company would be torn apart by the IRS, and Kuldell and the other Hughes Tool Company executives would lose their plum.

Howard Hughes's Houston lawyer contacted Noah Dietrick. Dietrick sent Kuldell a very important reassuring letter stating that Hughes had revised his will and that it "generously provided for all his top executives." There is no evidence that Hughes executed this will. In fact, Howard Hughes had, however, told the executives he had provided for them in the will. Noah Dietrick had his scheme for Kuldell, and Howard Hughes had his scheme for all the executives to keep them happy believers. The letter would probably have been very important evidence in the Howard Hughes estate trials, if it were true.

Noah Dietrick was the first of Hughes top executives to manipulate himself into power in the Hughes organization.

In fact, from the time he was hired by Hughes in 1925, he was consolidating his power.

Howard Hughes, only twenty-nine, early realized the dangers of wealth as well as the joy of controlling it. He became fearful of making a new will, lest greed would influence others to control him. By promising his executives partial ownership of Hughes Tool Company, he thought they would be true to him. Noah Dietrick was now afraid of Kuldell's favoritism with Hughes because Kuldell had saved the company during the depression by opening the Gulf Brewery Company in Houston.

Kuldell was a thorn in Dietrick's side, as Dietrick thought Kuldell was Hughes's favorite. The power struggle was on. Hughes sent Dietrick to Houston to live and keep watch over the company books.

About two years later Kuldell was fired.

The Growing European Unrest

Hughes was more determined than ever to pursue aircraft design and manufacture and become foremost in aircraft development. The U.S. Army Air Force was growing and ready to modernize with faster, safer combat planes. This was 1930. All air force aircraft design and parts were at Wright Field in Akron, Ohio. With the onset of the depression, in 1929, labor was cheap. By 1938 the manufacture of commercial aircraft in California was demanding every available man and woman for employment. The impending threat of war pressed all college men into ROTC (Reserve Officer Training Corps) for the air force and the army, and most were drafted on graduation.

Contracts were let to companies like Lockheed for its P-38, Douglas for its A-20, and Boeing for its B-17. Hughes had lost a contract for the *H-1* to Lockheed for its P-38. Howard

Howard Hughes and the Boeing former military pursuit plane. *(Wide World Photos)*

Hughes had lost favor with those in command at Wright Field and failed to sell the air force his *H-1*.

In 1932, Howard Hughes's ambitions and attention were focused on air speed. Through special arrangements with the air force he secured (bought?) an air force pursuit plane from the Department of Commerce for his *Hell's Angels* filming. He set to work rebuilding it into a racer. After reconditioning the plane, he took it up for a test, averaging 225 miles per hour. He entered a Miami air race on January 14, 1934, and won. Then his mind was set to race coast to coast.

The *H-1* was fast for short distances but was not a long-distance racer. He found a plane at Mine's Field near Inglewood that fit his predetermined need. This plane was a Northrup Gamma. The only obstacle in getting the Gamma was that it belonged to a young woman aviatrix who also had plans to set a new record in the Bendix Air Race.

Jacqueline Cochran was already an aviatrix of note and was in no mood to sell her airplane. She had come up the hard way. She had never seen or talked to Howard Hughes, but of course, she had heard of him. After weeks of Howard's persistent calls, and with her financial situation, she reluctantly sold her plane (a lease with option).

Hughes had his specialists convert the Northrup Gamma to suit his specifications for a long-distance high-speed flight. He, again, went to the federal government and somehow got special permission to use a 925 HP Wright Cyclone engine the Air Corps had developed for exclusive military use.

In 1935, the Gamma was ready, and on January 13, 1936, Howard took off. After climbing to 15,000 feet, he throttled back and proved his former belief that at high altitudes reducing carburation does not reduce speed.

In spite of bad weather and loss of instruments, he set a new cross-country record of nine hours, twenty-seven minutes, ten seconds. Hughes then set two more records, paying for the plane he had bought from Jackie. Then he sold it back to her for less than he paid. There was no explanation. He just wanted to do it. Really, he was satisfied with what he had learned about the plane to build a better one.

Now, back to remodeling his *H-1* racer for long-distance flying to try to break his own coast-to-coast record.

The remodeling made use of Hughes's observations during his previous flights. Some of his innovations included: longer, heavier wings, greater fuel capacity with lighter tanks, hydraulic seat adjustment, a solid plastic cover for the cockpit, and an oxygen supply system with a tube to the cockpit.

While his specialists fitted his *H-1* for the cross-country race, he became acquainted with Katharine Hepburn. Of course, there were other women on the side, but Kate was his favorite. After three years together she kissed him good-bye.

August 18, 1938: Hughes's First Test of the H-1

The *H-1* easily flew at 300 miles per hour, so instead of entering the National Air Races, Howard had a bigger goal. He knew he could easily win the air race. His sights were first set on the speed record over a measured course, yet he had in mind the California to New York transcontinental flight record now held by Col. Roscoe Turner, a former pilot of *Hell's Angels*. Turner's record was ten hours, two minutes, fifty-seven seconds. Hughes's impressive *H-1* records of 355, 339, 351, and 340 miles per hour in the measured course were observed by Amelia Earhart. The flight ended in a beet field, a crash landing without injury.

While testing his plane, he discovered that his speed instrument accurately recorded speed at sea level, not higher altitudes. In other words, the higher the altitude, the faster the travel, with less resistance and less fuel. Discovery of these facts revolutionized the future of aircraft design.

On January 18, 1937, Howard flew the *Silver Bullet* (as the *H-1* was now called) cross country to Newark, New Jersey, encountering foul weather. Hughes knew the weather was unseasonably bad for this time of year but had worked long and hard engineering his plane for such an occurrence. However, it nearly caused a fatal ending. Nevertheless, he flew over Newark Airport in a record seven hours, twenty-eight minutes, twenty-five seconds, at an average of 332 miles per hour. Noisy crowds awaited him, but true to his nature, he was desperate to escape their flashing cameras and interrogatives.

Wiley Post, Amelia Earhart, Jacqueline Cochran, et al., now admired Howard Hughes as an accomplished and famous aviator. Pres. Franklin D. Roosevelt honored him at the White House and remarked that he would like to fly with him. Howard Hughes was unimpressed, but not too shy to already have plans to sell pursuit planes to the U.S. Air Force.

Howard Hughes had visions of a larger plane than the ones flown around the world by Wiley Post. He wanted to produce an airplane that was larger, carried a full crew, and was safe for flying over water. He chose the Sikorsky S-43, a large amphibian two-engine cantilever plane (a plane whose wings had no external supports). In 1937, he applied to the Bureau of Air Commerce in Washington for permission to make the around-the-world flight. He was turned down, for fear it would end up in a crash, as Hughes's former Sikorsky had. He was turned down because the bureau did not think his plane was worthy of the expense for aircraft science.

The next year (1938), he reapplied and was again turned down, because an S-43 had just crashed and had not been investigated.

He quickly changed his plans and received permission to buy a new Lockheed passenger plane, the Lockheed 14.

Hughes Aircraft made substantial changes in the Lockheed 14 to meet Hughes's specifications for his around-the-world dream plane. The most significant change was the plane's engines. He fitted his new plane with two supercharged Wright G-102 engines. His engineers installed an automatic pilot and various navigational instruments, etc., not used by Lindbergh in his Atlantic flight.

Hughes's *H-1* (the *Winged Bullet*) now had many features and improvements developed by Hughes and his engineers. It would be the first pursuit plane of the air force with cantilever wings. However, the air force did not buy it, probably because of Hughes's failure to keep an appointment in Dayton, Ohio, with Maj. Gen. Oliver P. Echols for the plane's demonstration. Howard was supposed to fly the plane to Wright Field (Dayton) and be met by General Echols and the top air force delegation. He had become too busy designing a larger plane for an around-the-world record, thus saw no reason to fly his *Winged Bullet* to Dayton.

The Katharine Hepburn Story

According to Katharine Hepburn's book *Me*, the three years she and Howard lived together were possibly their best. They both loved nature, golfing, flying, and swimming.

Katharine Hepburn has been and is very independent and straightforward. She had her ups and downs as an actress before she met Howard Hughes. Her first incident with Howard Hughes was while she and Cary Grant were shooting a picture at the beach. Howard Hughes surprised the group by landing in a field near their lunch spot and joined the group for lunch. Kate did not much like the intrusion.

Later, while golfing at Bel Air Country Club, Howard landed on the fairway and finished the nine with Kate and friends. Howard ordered his men to dismantle the plane and remove it immediately.

Later, in Boston, Howard moved into the same hotel where Kate was staying and she had supper with him.

Katharine Hepburn stated that she thought Howard's deafness was largely responsible for his later problems.

Then, while both Howard and Kate were in Chicago, there were rumors. Newspapers headlined: "Hughes and Katharine Hepburn Will Marry Today."

Katharine Hepburn and Howard Hughes "drifted

along," enjoying each other's company, playing golf, etc. Howard was a good, but slow golfer, Kate a good but faster golfer. They enjoyed flying and landing on Long Island Sound. They especially enjoyed skinny-dipping off the airplane's wing.

Howard Hughes's priority had been and still was his *H-1* project, in preparation for his cross-country record in his own plane. He remodeled and renamed the *H-1* the *Winged Bullet*. During his preparations and flying back and forth from California to Long Island, he crashed his seaplane (not the *H-1 Winged Bullet*) into Long Island Sound. This was his third aircraft accident. He emerged uninjured.

Howard taught Katharine Hepburn to fly. She became as much a stunt pilot as Howard. One time she took off alone under New York's Fifty-ninth Street Bridge. Howard was preparing to leave on his around-the-world flight.

Howard Hughes and Katharine Hepburn never married. They each had their separate lives and stubbornness. They were content together for three wonderful years. They separated as friends with different priorities. Katharine Hepburn was rapid-fire; her career was most important and needed no support. Howard Hughes was slow and deaf; his career was most important and needed support.

He was not too shy to approach the air force to promote his *Winged Bullet* as a new pursuit army plane. It was first refused as inadequate without some improvements. The air force then offered to survey his plane at Wright Field, Ohio. Howard Hughes failed to keep the appointment with Maj. Gen. Oliver P. Echols. Hughes was again in San Limbo.

Hughes then went to work in earnest on his project, his famous around-the-world flight in his Sikorski S-43 two-engine amphibian plane. His plan was to show the world that a properly built and piloted airplane could circle the globe without problems and that this feat would raise the curtain to regular commercial around-the-world flights. He was refused permission to make the flight by the Bureau of Air Commerce in Washington.

A second request was about to be approved when some other S-43 crashed.

Hughes heard of a new plane, built by Lockheed, the Lockheed 14 about to be tested. He prevailed on Lockheed and secured the first plane and immediately made several changes for increased safety and distance worthy of the 15,000-mile around-the-world trip. He installed an automatic pilot (an innovation) and various pressure and temperature gauges.

Howard's Around-the-World Flight

Before taking to flight on his around-the-world exploit, Howard Hughes wrote another will and testament, virtually the same as his earlier one. He had become concerned after Amelia Earhart's mysterious disappearance near the end of her around-the-world flight. This will was placed in safe deposit box #3102 in the First National Bank of Houston, Texas, but was never found.

Late in the day, July 10, 1938, Hughes and his crew were ready for their flight to Floyd Bennett Field in New York, where they would take off on their around-the-world record-seeking flight. They were met at Floyd Bennett Field by Grover Whalen and a huge crowd. Grover Whalen had a ceremony for Howard Hughes and christened the plane *The New York World's Fair 1939*. Howard accepted the honor dressed in his familiar social attire—rumpled trousers, white shirt, no tie, and the always-brown fedora. He was embarrassed by all the commotion over him. He gave a brief speech from a rumpled

The Lockheed 14 above Manhattan on a test run before the world flight, July 1938. *(United Press International)*

note he rummaged from his trousers, apologizing for being impolite, and slipped away.

That evening, 7:19 P.M., he gunned the plane and took off in a cloud of dust. He "dipped the wings" over Katharine Hepburn's old home, and they were on their way.

Until this time, ocean flying had not been carefully studied. Howard Hughes and his engineers spent many months studying and improving the technicalities of such a hazardous endeavor. He set up elaborate radio-to-ship communications.

The first mishap occurred when he lost radio contact for an hour and a half.

They encountered strong winds and storms that caused increased fuel consumption to maintain proper speed for the heavy aircraft. There was worry about reaching Paris before running out of fuel. However, a tail wind developed and they made it to Paris.

The route taken was over Boston, Nova Scotia, Cape Breton Island, Newfoundland, and then to Paris. Foul weather and headwinds over the Atlantic caused much concern. Howard feared the plane would run out of gas. They arrived in Paris in sixteen hours, thirty-eight minutes. Then on to Moscow, arriving at 11:15 A.M. the next day. They arrived at Omsk in Siberia at night and then ten and one half hours later at Yakutak. The next day, July 13, they landed at Fairbanks, Alaska. They refueled at Minneapolis, Minnesota, and then on to New York LaGuardia Field. Mayor LaGuardia gave a welcome, saying seven million New Yorkers congratulated him. While a guest of Grover Whalen, in his home, Howard Hughes escaped and went to see Katharine Hepburn at her Turtle Bay home, leaving hundreds of lookie-loos and cameramen standing in front.

In the East he was honored with parades and finally flew his *The New York World's Fair 1939* to Houston where he visited his aunts and friends. Governor James V. Allred introduced him to an overflow crowd at a banquet, extolling his great accomplishments as a veteran flyer. Hughes said he could not even get a job as a "First Pilot." He didn't have the two years to spend as a "Second Pilot" apprentice.

Next day he and his two aunts, Annette Lummis and Martha Houstoun, paid a rare visit to his Hughes Tool Company.

He left the following day for Los Angeles on his silver

Lockheed H I (*World's Fair 1939*), never to see his relatives again.

Jim Haworth in the Forties

During the late thirties, Jim Haworth was finishing high school at Moapa Valley High. Fun with the girls and athletics was drawing to a close. He became especially interested in Iris. She was not eighteen yet, and they decided to get married anyhow. In June of 1939 Jim took her to Kingman, Arizona, and married her on June 23. Jim still has her. They worked around the Moapa Valley for about a year. Then, in 1940, Jim found out the Warm Springs Ranch (then called the Home Ranch) was for lease. Iris and he leased it for five years from Mrs. Mary Hawkins and Mrs. Ray Weber, the daughters who had inherited the ranch from Fitzgerald.

First Few Years with Home Ranch

They finally settled on a lease of the Home Ranch for $2,500 for five years.

Soon after they moved onto the Home Ranch, a man, a Mr. Griffith, owner of the Last Frontier Hotel, bought the last two years of the five-year lease from Jim. Jim also leased the Livingston Ranch (Hidden Valley Ranch). In 1942, he no more than got started on the Livingston Ranch when Mr. Griffith decided he would raise his own beef and, before Jim knew it, outright bought the Livingston Ranch and the Home Ranch. After this, Jim managed both ranches for Mr. Griffith.

Also, Jim and Iris's son, Jerry, was born that year, officiated by their friend, Dr. Gilbert.

Early in 1943, the Haworths moved to Coos Bay, Oregon.

They couldn't stand the cold and rain after their desert lives, so they moved back to Fallon, Nevada, and bought a home. They sold their Fallon home and bought a new home in Las Vegas. In 1944, and before they got settled, Jim was called into the navy. Imagine a Nevada desert cowboy in the navy. They knew he was a good rescue swimmer. They had heard of his daring swimming and diving episode in 1941.

Then Jim and Iris's daughter, Rita, was born.

Jim spent six months in the navy until the war ended. His navy job was swabbing the decks.

Iris kept busy at their Las Vegas home caring for Jerry and baby Rita.

After Jim was mustered out of the navy, Iris and he went in as partners with L. R. Ivans in the dairy business in the Moapa Valley. They bought a small ranch there and sold their Las Vegas home. It didn't take long to find out that their arrangement in the dairy business was not for them. They were starving on just milk for a diet. They all needed more than that. Jim sold his interest in the dairy and went to work in construction to iron out the wrinkles in his stomach.

After working in construction until 1952, Jim went to work for a rich New Yorker named Frank Taylor, who came to Nevada and bought the Home Ranch and built a six-bedroom, six-bath mansion for his wife.

The Frank Taylor mansion on the Warm Springs Ranch.

4
The War Years

The Magic Hands of Jim Haworth
Characterization by Iris Haworth

Jim Haworth is small in stature and prematurely gray. An iron gray mustache gives him a dignified look. His cowboy hat is saturated with sweat and covered with many layers of dust. His spurs that have tickled the ribs of many horses have never been taken from his boots.

Though Jim is nice looking, he wouldn't take a beauty prize. The wind and the sun have tanned his face, and his calloused hands are seared brown. Even though his fingers have been broken and bent out of shape, there is something distinctive about his hands. They are capable; they have worked on the machinery and taken care of and operated on sick cows and horses. They handle a rope with accuracy and when needed prepare a good meal. In the quiet of the evening they sketch the incidents of the day. Truly, they are the hands of an artist.

Of Jim's many virtues, the three outstanding qualities are honesty, determination, and capability. He was always called on to help in any emergency. Oh, that terrible flood disaster.

The Flood of August '41

It was right after Iris and Jim leased and left their Hidden Valley Ranch and moved to the Home Ranch. He helped rescue people caught in the flood. On of the worst flash floods in history had risen to twelve feet across the Las Vegas-to-Utah highway.

At the time Jim was over there near Glendale, Nevada, with his team, working on the highway for the road department.

That morning, August 12, 1941, was when he got there. A workman for the road department rushed over to where Jim was taking care of the horses. He said, "The flood has washed out the road and there are people stranded."

Jim gathered up the reins, tied the horses to a tree on the bank, and beat it over to the place where the road was submerged under eight feet of water and another twelve-foot wall of water was crashing down. Some workmen were caught in it and were never found. By that time cars were backed up fifteen miles both ways. They waited a bit on the bank, waiting for the water to go down a little. The water was already shoulder-deep at this spot and there was a car in it.

They were up on the bank when the twelve-foot wall of water rushed them. It just picked that car up and took it down the country, swirling around in the wash. There must have been two hundred or three hundred people on the bank, and nobody had guts enough to jump into that damn torrent of water, only Jim, and he was used to it maybe. The car was floating away with a woman and kid, so he dove in there and got alongside the car and kept it from turning over and got the woman to finally hand him the kid out the window and swam ashore with him and then went back to that car, which was still going down country.

The water was going through the windows, and the car

was completely underwater. Jim managed to dive down and open a door, and the woman came out on top of his head. He finally got the woman under control and started to shore with her. One of the highway men threw a long rope out to Jim and pulled them in. A lot of newsmen contacted Jim about the rescue.

The Second World War

The Second World War broke out in September 1939. Hughes then designed his medium-range bomber. It would fly 450 miles per hour and carry a crew of five. With his lack of experience in aircraft design, this was another new venture (adventure) for Howard Hughes and his neophyte Hughes Aircraft Company. This plane was not only a new design, but was to be made of plywood used elsewhere in duromold process. The air force refused a contract because of its claim that wood would absorb moisture and crack and shatter.

True to Hughes's secrecy, he would not allow inspection of his design but corresponded with Wright Field, urging consideration of his new plane. Finally, high-ranking officers, headed by Gen. H. H. (Hap) Arnold, flew to Hughes Aircraft Company to meet with Hughes and inspect the plane. Hughes was not present. No one knew where he was. He was said to be in San Limbo. His guards refused entry into the plant, even to the chief of the air force. The officers, in disgust, flew back to Washington. It seemed that Howard Hughes had several other irons in the fire that occupied his valuable time. His principal interest at the time was his hobby of producing movies, especially *The Outlaw* with Jane Russell, exposing her breasts. He even invented a special bra with a string to pull at the proper time.

Now, in 1940, he was working day and night on his D-2

project, as well as movies. He was also embroiled in acquiring control of Transcontinental and Western Airlines (TWA).

He spared no expense in proceeding with the D-2. He purchased 1,300 acres near Culver City and moved his Hughes Aircraft plant from Burbank into the new 60,000-square-foot plant. The outside workers graded and paved a 9,000-foot runway. By 1941, Hughes Aircraft had one hundred engineers and four hundred other employees. Hughes had problems getting the right wood, glue, and other materials, plus spare parts, propellers, engines, etc. The engine to be used had been assigned by Wright Field to other manufacturers.

The Kaiser-Hughes Flying Boat

Henry Kaiser, the former shipbuilder, presented a plan to build super cargo planes to fly over the submarine menace. He lured Howard Hughes into a partnership whereby Hughes would design and engineer 500 planes and Kaiser would build them and have them delivered in ten months. Howard Hughes voiced his reluctance to go ahead, knowing they could not be produced in ten months. However, he agreed to go ahead.

In late 1941, Kaiser again went to Washington with plans for the colossal Kaiser-Hughes flying boat. This time he called on Jesse Jones, owner of the Reconstruction Finance Corp. (RFC), to encourage Donald Nelson, Chairman of the War Production Board, to endorse the project. Donald Nelson knew the project had many Washington supporters. RFC was awarded financing for the flying boat.

Eighteen months was the time authorized to build three planes, and neither Kaiser nor Hughes would receive a profit. Now Howard Hughes was on the threshold of becoming a major airplane manufacturer.

On September 27, Merrill C. Meigs, deputy director of the War Production Board, talked with Hughes about the plane. Hughes was sure he could not produce the plane in less than two years. Meigs agreed that it was impossible and that all of Washington knew it.

On November 16, 1942, the contract was signed for the K-H flying boat. No aircraft engineers had ever designed a 200-ton, ten-story-high aircraft, and now Howard, with limited aircraft design experience, was about to built one of wood. At this point Hughes Aircraft Company was composed of only about two hundred men. Every employee reported directly to Howard Hughes. His chief engineers worked at the plant daytimes and met nights with Hughes at his new rented home in Bel Air. Oftentimes Howard was not home. He escaped to tend to his movies and women.

In spring of 1943, the air force decided to buy the previously rejected Sikorsky S-43 for transporting army engineers to isolated new air bases. Howard had made a few improvements on the S-43, hoping to use it on his around-the-world flight.

CAA officials arrived to approve the K-H plane, the most incredible aircraft contract ever designed. The flying boat was known by the government as Plancor 1424 (H-K1). Hughes and Kaiser called it the Hercules. In a short time it was commonly called the Spruce Goose or the Wooden Goose, much to Howard Hughes's dismay.

Howard Hughes was again in his San Limbo. He was invited to a Santa Barbara birthday party for Katharine Hepburn. In his state of stress, his top aircraft engineers, Whitaker and Rockefeller, were called on to drive him from Los Angeles. On the way, an injured dog was seen along the highway. Hughes ordered the driver to stop and pick up the dog. As soon as they reached Santa Barbara, they took the dog to an emergency veterinarian. Howard left the party twice to inquire

The Hercules (Spruce Goose) under construction. *(Contractors Cargo Company Photo)*

about the dog's condition. His compassion was always greater for animals than for humans.

On the CAA officials' arrival at Hughes Aircraft, Howard was nowhere to be found. He was flying over Lake Mead and practicing takeoffs and landings with his S-43 on the water.

Discovery of Moapa Valley

This was one of the times Howard flew alone over the

Moapa Indian Reservation and Moapa Valley, forty-five miles northeast of Las Vegas. He became enthralled with the idea that he would buy a ranch in that beautiful valley for his permanent secluded home and enjoy his solitude with nature.

He was happy to escape from Culver City and its problems and enjoy his S-43 flights over the desert and blue Lake Mead. Each time he circled and headed for Boulder City on Lake Mead, he closely observed the almost-hidden valley with the acres of green pastures, trees, and a beautiful estate mansion. He spent his nights in the city of Las Vegas, which was now attracting big-time gamblers, showgirls and, of course, the enterprising Mafia. His days were spent flying, landing, and taxiing on an inlet of the huge lake. Admirers and reporters with their cameras were out there in everything from barges and speedboats to rowboats, trying to get a glimpse of the fabulous Hughes and his revolutionary plane.

Howard refuted the idea of hiring someone to do his solo testing, saying, "Hell, I'd miss all the fun."

On May 16, 1943, Charles W. Von Rosenberg, a CAA test pilot, and his assistants met Hughes at Boulder City to make tests of the S-43 on water. Of course, Howard insisted on piloting the plane. Von Rosenberg was copilot. William M. "Coco" Cline, a CAA inspector; Gene Blandford, Hughes's flight test engineer; and Richard Felt, Hughes's mechanic, made up the flight crew.

After a very comfortable flight, Rosenberg asked Hughes to land on the lake and turn the controls over to him. Howard very precipitously guided the heavy plane down to the water, touched down smoothly, and, at ninety miles per hour, splashed through the water, when the S-43 suddenly nosed over, skidded sideways, and crashed, with pieces of fuselage, wing, and parts flying everywhere. Waist-deep in the sinking plane, all but the CAA inspector survived. He was never found. This was Hughes's fourth plane crash. In each instance he knew the fault and corrected it. In the case of the S-43, it was the only time that Howard Hughes did not personally check every detail before flying. His ground crew at the Boulder City airfield had carelessly loaded the plane with uneven load balance, causing the nose-over and skidding wreck.

There was discontent at the Culver City Hughes Aircraft plant. The flying boat was further and further behind schedule. It seemed no one was interested in the project. In ten months $6 million of the $9.8 million of the government contract had been spent; three months later the Hughes general manager and his department heads quit.

The work on the flying boat had to wait further. Hughes was contacted by General Arnold and Col. Elliot Roosevelt to build reconnaissance planes. The makeshift models in use were not efficient. Hughes assigned his public relations man, John W. Meyer, to entertain Colonel Roosevelt and sell him the D-2 contract. Meyer and Colonel Roosevelt had been friends earlier, when Meyer was popular with the movie set. The D-2, a wooden model, had been tested but performed poorly, and Hughes sent it back to the shop for important changes.

Meyer threw parties and tours of the studios for Colonel Roosevelt and his officers, introducing Colonel Roosevelt to Faye Emerson. Howard Hughes personally showed the plane to Colonel Roosevelt and his officers. Hughes was awarded the contract for 100 XF-11s (D-2s).

There was much dissent in the air force concerning the XF-11 purchase. Also, the production of the flying boat was halted. Hughes went to Washington and pleaded his case (cases). He was so adept in the hearings that general sentiment was that he was the wronged party.

The Hercules flying boat contract for three planes was canceled, and a new contract for one plane at $18 million was issued.

Hughes hired executives with promises to give them huge salaries and thousands of shares of TWA. Then he reneged and hired others, who also quit. Constant problems in his aircraft plant, his movie business, and Hughes Aircraft were taxing his mental and physical health. He started and didn't finish dozens of memoranda. This was 1943. Hughes again disappeared into seclusion, his San Limbo.

Before disappearing, Hughes confidentially assigned Nadine Henley (his private secretary) to write a new will, place it in a Romaine Street safe, and wear the key around her neck. He never doubted her abilities and honesty. Their relationship was purely business. After Hughes's breakdown and disappearance in 1944, no one knew of his whereabouts for many months, except a mechanic at Hughes Aircraft who, years later, said he and Howard Hughes shuttled from Las Vegas to Palm Springs and Reno under assumed names and doing no work. They flew over Howard Hughes's new other empire. He was happy in his dreams of living there.

During the 1940's, Howard Hughes continued his "collection" of famed actresses. He commissioned Bill Gay to hire them for little pay with promises of their starring in his coming movies. Bill Gay happily provided them with lavish hotel suites and expensive clothes. They were closely guarded and could not leave their suites. This caper of Howard's was called the Hughes Purdah.

The Senate Investigation of the Near Fatal XF-11 Crash

During Hughes's San Limbo, one-time vice president of production of Consolidated Vultee Aircraft, Chuck Perelle took over the Hughes Aircraft Division as general manager. The XF-11 (Spruce Goose) was far behind schedule and the air force had threatened cancellation before Hughes hired Perelle.

Perelle found a worse situation than expected. There was complete inefficiency and lack of knowledge and experience throughout the aircraft plant. Hughes promised Perelle stock options (as he had other executives, including Noah Dietrick) and complete authority over Hughes Aircraft. The other Houston executives and Noah Dietrick, worried over Perelle's authority and their vulnerability, sought to rid the company of Perelle. However, Perelle did straighten out the aircraft operation and even arranged a $1.5 million loan from RFC to move the 200-ton Hercules (Spruce Goose) from Culver City to Long Beach Harbor. Hughes refused the deal because it was giving the government, not him, control over testing the plane. He wanted to finish his promise to fly the Spruce Goose and retire to his million-acre desert oasis.

In spite of Perelle's efforts the contract for the D-3 fell far behind schedule and the government canceled the 200-plane contract and renewed for only 2 more planes and no more military aircraft manufacture to be granted to Hughes. Hughes instead financed a fleet of TWA passenger planes, without Perelle's consent. Perelle confronted Hughes and Hughes fired him, even though he had accomplished a lot in the aircraft division for Hughes. Dietrick's power worries were over for the time being. Howard Hughes was in a constant state of manic depression and drug addiction, but his determination to fly the Spruce Goose and live on his ranch remained.

In June 1946, costing $80,000, the parts of the behemoth boat prototype were transported to Long Beach Harbor.

Hughes went ahead with his XF-11, preparing for its test flight. He was again personally supervising the completion of his XF-11 and testing on the runway.

The XF-11 tested by Howard Hughes alone ended in a

very nearly fatal crash through houses in Hollywood. He was rescued from the burning plane by a nearby army sergeant. Hughes was blamed by the air force for his nearly fatal accident because of not following air force test rules (flight time, emergency radio contact, etc.). After his recovery, Hughes blamed and sued Hamilton-Standard, manufacturer of the defective right rear (contrarotating) propeller that had broken a seal, leaked oil, and gone into reverse.

Dr. Vernon R. Mason cared for Hughes during his recovery and kept him supplied with morphine for pain. Howard was taken from morphine and given codeine on demand.

This was the beginning of Howard Hughes's fateful slow death from narcoticism.

After the crash, Hughes flew his converted B-23 (XF-11) bomber to prove to himself that he was not afraid to fly again. He again enjoyed his flights over his million-acre hideaway. He now grew a mustache to cover scars on his lip suffered from the accident.

He convinced Lt. Gen. Ira C. Eaker to make an appeal to Commanding Gen. Carl Spaatz for permission to test fly the new and improved XF-11. Nine months later (September 1947), Ira Eaker became vice president of Hughes Aircraft.

During the XF-11 episode, the Senate Defense Program Investigation Committee was quietly probing into Hughes's flying boat and reconnaissance plane contracts.

Still another iron in the fire was Hughes's ownership of TWA and his being awarded CAA approval for overseas passenger routes, competing against Pan American. Then (1946) Congress introduced a bill to consolidate overseas airlines, leaving TWA without the overseas routes.

Sen. Ralph Owen Brewster (the Pan American–hired senior Republican Senator), author of the bill, was also in charge of the bill. Howard Hughes's lobbyists defeated the bill.

However, Senator Brewster's power was again a thorn in Howard Hughes's flesh when he became chairman of the Senate Special Committee Investigating the National Defense Program. On January 23, 1947, Brewster announced his investigation of the Hercules flying boat contracts.

Pan Am's senatorial agent was trying to hurt TWA by embarrassing Hughes. Senate investigators were sent to Los Angeles to probe into the business of Hughes Aircraft Company. Hughes refused examination of the company's books until threatened with a subpoena. The committee had already obtained information that Hughes had entertained Col. Elliott Roosevelt, who recommended the XF-11 project while most of the air force was against it. The Republican committee would have been delighted to embarrass the Roosevelts.

On April 5, 1947, Howard Hughes successfully flew the XF-11 and emerged as one of the largest government-financed airplane makers.

When Brewster, at the hearings, accused Hughes of payoffs, Hughes retorted with, "What about the two airplanes you bummed off me? What about those Pan American trips you took to South America?"

When the hearings became more serious. Hughes took the stand and eloquently told of his months of personally working and supervising the production of the biggest airplane in the world, which would transport many hundreds of passengers and hundreds of tons of war material across the ocean. He explained that it was a prototype and that it was the first in the evolution of huge transports overseas and it might not fly, but the knowledge from it would revolutionize air traffic. Sen. Homer Ferguson, chairman of the War Investigation Subcommittee, became rattled at the testimony of Hughes and adjourned the meeting to a later time. Howard Hughes accused him of being a coward not to stand and face the music. Hughes felt vindicated as the reporters and photographers applauded. However, it was learned that his hotel suite had been bugged and this added to Hughes's paranoia and fear of being spied upon.

He flew back to Los Angeles in his converted D-2 bomber, also planning to aggressively complete and fly his Hercules flying boat.

November 1, 1947, crowds of press reporters and photographers were on hand to see the first and only flight of the Hercules. They were overwhelmed at the size of this giant airplane.

> Built to carry 700 passengers or a load of 60 tons, the Hercules seemed more a creation of science fiction than the work of man's flesh and blood. The tail was as tall as an eight story building. The wingspan, more than double that of a B-29, was longer than a football field. The propellers were 17 feet in diameter. The hull stood 30 feet tall. The wings were so thick a man could stand up in them.

Hughes taxied the plane on Long Beach Harbor several times and, on the last trial run for the day, decided to put it in the air. He flew it at about seventy feet above water for a mile, then set it down.

Hughes was quiet about his accomplishment, knowing that the Hercules would not fly again without more powerful engines, which were not available at that time. He obtained a right from the RFC to lease the Hercules from the government for $450,000 a year. He had additional expenses in leasing the site from Long Beach and maintaining an air-conditioned humidity-controlled hangar, all costing Howard Hughes about $1 million a year.

The XF-11 bomber was turned over to the air force late in 1947. On July 26, 1949, it was ordered cut up for scrap. It had not met expectations.

Howard Hughes ended the war years fraught with disappointment with the air force and the government. His ambitious dreams of being a major producer of superior aircraft for defense and war effort ended with the air force change of plans. He had suffered such stresses as manic depression and drug addiction. His notoriety had caused him to seek seclusion from the press and government agents.

He was a public hero for what he had accomplished with his millions for his own satisfaction, at the risk of his life. Although his aircraft manufacturing enterprise was put to rest, his knowledge and technical expertise had produced innovations that helped revolutionize the aircraft industry. His Hercules, commonly called the Spruce Goose, the forty-ton woodpile, etc., was, in fact, a reality—the biggest, heaviest aircraft in history—and he did, in fact, fly it himself. It was a prototype that he accomplished with all the powers biting at his heels. He knew it would not be a practical huge transport with the power of the engines of that day. He demonstrated that an aircraft could and would be produced to transport hundreds of passengers around the world. He was proud of his accomplishment and was glad to show the Spruce Goose to the public.

A Change of Life—Mormon Aides Exposed

Late in 1947, Hughes decided to temporarily ease off his previous goal, that of becoming the biggest airplane manufacturer. He would continue Romaine Street as the command center but would hire a man to be his man—to see that his orders were carried out. No longer would he bite the bullet at Romaine Street. Nadine Henley, his faithful executive secretary, who had hired Frank William Gay for part-time office work, suggested Bill Gay for the job. Gay had four years of

Brigham Young University business school and was aiming at a degree from Columbia to become a college professor. He had been brought up as a Mormon.

In December 1947, Hughes interviewed and hired Gay as his administrative assistant. Gay organized a second-floor message center at Romaine Street. He hired Mormon college students to man the center twenty-four hours a day. Gay assumed charge of Howard Hughes's other empire and his man and issued orders from Romaine Street. More experienced subordinates of Hughes now received fewer direct orders from Hughes, and Gay was careful not to intimidate these older employees.

This arrangement left Hughes free to get back to his moviemaking hobby and his other empire. Hughes did not know that Gay was wheeling and dealing with his money for himself. Of course, Hughes intended that each of his empires, whether hobby or not, was to be profitable and tax-deductible and satisfying to his personal accomplishment and control.

Howard Hughes was now residing in the top suite of the Old Flamingo Hotel with "Big" Levine, the bell captain, his orderly.[1] Big Levine related that his job for Hughes was maintaining Hughes's stable of actresses who lived at the hotel.

Hughes's new goal was to gain control of RKO studios and theaters. Hughes heard that RKO was for sale. With many meetings at Floyd Odlum's 900-acre Indio (near Palm Springs) Ranch, Hughes matched wits with the masterful president of Atlas Corporation, which had grown from a single investment by Odlum to a huge conglomerate of profitable companies, RKO being one of them. Hughes finally bought 24 percent of RKO and control of its operations. There were several years of huge losses, but Hughes doggedly remained the ultimate boss of every detail, even the movie *The Las Vegas Story*, starring the half-naked Jane Russell.

He became embroiled in the anticommunist investigations in Hollywood by firing his writer of *The Las Vegas Story* when Paul Jerrico refused to answer to the Senate Anti-Communist Activity Committee. Although Howard Hughes had never voted in any political election, he was always strongly against communism.

Once again, Hughes defending his rights gained wide public and Republican support for his stand. He won the case brought against him by Paul Jerrico and the Screen Writers Guild for breach of contract. However, the RKO studios continued to lose millions and Hughes sold RKO to a syndicate made up of several shady investors.

Summary of the Forties: Howard Hughes and His First Glimpse of the Warm Springs Ranch

While Jim and Iris Haworth in 1940 were leasing the Warm Springs Ranch from Mrs. Mary Hawkins and Mrs. Ray Weber (daughters of Fitzgerald), Howard Hughes was busy redesigning his H-1 airplane, which set a new cross-country speed record in 7 hours, 28 minutes, and 2 seconds, at an average of 332 miles per hour. He was more interested in improving design and function than fame.

The late thirties and 1940s were the principal years of Howard Hughes's Purdah, his romance with Katharine Hepburn, and his spree of hiring actress beauties for his movies. Most of his actresses never appeared in his films but were held "captive" in luxurious hotel suites. He was intent on acquiring, keeping, and guarding an actress just to know he owned the best. Some he never saw because they were "bought" for him by William Gay, who was at the time his trusted top man. Of course, Gay overextended his authority and enjoyed the ladies' roundup. William Gay had come up from being an office boy in the Hughes Aircraft Company, and now, he was suddenly living a fabulous life, courtesy of Howard Hughes.

Howard Hughes's executive secretary, Nadine Henley, urged Hughes to put Gay in command as Hughes's man when Howard Hughes was suffering from his first stress depression syndrome.

In 1941, Howard Hughes was contacted by Henry Kaiser and urged to join with him in designing a super transport plane to replace ships for overseas transport of military troops. The transport ships were being sunk at will by U-2 submarines. Howard Hughes was to engineer and design the planes, and together he and Kaiser would build them. Kaiser backed out of the deal in 1942, and Hughes took the ball to the U.S. Air Force for approval and funds. This was the beginning of the ill-fated Hughes Hercules (Spruce Goose) project.

In 1942, Mr. Griffith, owner of Frontier Hotel, bought the Warm Springs Home Ranch and the Livingston Ranch.

Johnny Jones, an ex–American Airlines pilot, became Howard Hughes's double, to be seen where Hughes wanted publicity. This was the time of Howard Hughes's Purdah and his romance of several years with Katharine Hepburn. Although the news media pronounced a date they would marry, neither of them intended that course. They enjoyed each other's company and living together, but each had his or her own career and, with their similar personalities, they went their own way with Howard in command.

Their intimate life was principally in and about Howard's airplanes. He taught Katharine to fly and they enjoyed his seaplane flights, landing at the eastern beaches and skinny-dipping off the wing on Long Island Sound. One time Katharine took off alone from under New York's 59th Street Bridge.

Jim Haworth, at this time, was leasing the Warm Springs Ranch (called the Home Ranch). His lease was from the two sisters, Mrs. Mary Hawkins and Mrs. Ray Weber. The last two years of the five-year lease were bought from Jim by the Frontier Hotel.

In August 1941, Jim performed his miraculous life-saving feat during the Moapa flood disaster. The story was carried in the *Las Vegas Review* on August 12, 1941.

In 1942, with the World War II in full swing, Jim and Iris had their personal worries. What was to be their fate? Iris was pregnant, and Jim was subject to the draft. The year wore on and Jerry was born. With the pressure of uncertainty, both Jim and Iris became depressed and temporarily moved to Coos Bay, Oregon. In 1943, they returned to Nevada and purchased a home in Las Vegas. Daughter Rita was born in 1944, soon after Jim enlisted in the navy.

Howard Hughes, along with his Purdah, Katharine Hepburn, the Spruce Goose project, and his other pending Hughes Aircraft projects, was accumulating more and more TWA stock until, in 1944, he owned 44 percent of TWA. TWA had become the favorite of all his projects. He bought more planes for TWA and was competing with Pan Am for overseas routes. Pan Am became worried about the rapid growth of TWA and later sponsored a bill in Congress, through a favored congressman, to consolidate overseas airlines and leave TWA out. Howard Hughes found it necessary to use his congressional influence to prevent this unfair bill from passage.

In 1943, while Howard Hughes was flying his D-2 seaplane from Lake Mead, he circled the Moapa Valley and spotted the Home Ranch, which immediately became his dream hideaway retirement home, away from the spying IRS and nosy public. Since a young man, observing with his father a seaplane take off, he had wanted to build and fly one of his own, hence his introduction into the aircraft industry.

On May 16, 1943, Howard Hughes had his accident on Lake Mead with his D-2 seaplane while demonstrating it to the

CAB (Civil Aeronautics Board). The fault was that of his ground crew, who had not prepared the plane properly for the flight. The air force was contracting for manufacture of many D-2s for reconnaissance missions.

Now, more problems were confronting Hughes.

The year 1947 was probably Howard Hughes's most stressful one. January 23 was the start of the Brewster Congressional hearings investigating the Hercules (Spruce Goose) flying boat contract. Hughes proved its ability to fly on November 1 at Long Beach, California. Although many called it a farce, Howard Hughes had always maintained that it was a prototype with underpowered engines and a breakthrough for huge planes to come. It remains the largest airplane ever built. He pioneered the practicability of transport seaplanes to carry hundreds of passengers worldwide.

After the hearings, Howard Hughes proceeded with his D-2 conversion, preparing to seek a new around-the-world record.

In 1947, due to Howard Hughes's successful XF-11 (fighter) contract, he became the U.S.'s largest subsidized aircraft manufacturer.

It was in December 1947, Howard Hughes designated his courier, William Gay, on recommendation from Nadine Henley, his man to run all operations from his 7000 Romaine Street, Los Angeles, inner-sanctum message center for control of his executives. Howard Hughes never gave anyone full authority to operate and manage his various ventures. The nearest to full authority was held by Jim Haworth with Hughes's million-acre Warm Springs Ranch and ranges. William Gay intercepted all of Hughes's messages to Jim Haworth. Jim met monthly with Gay and his executives at the Romaine Street address, not knowing that Gay was making the rules. One time Howard Hughes heard of Jim's manuscript for the book *The Other Empire,* and requested it. Jim quickly obliged but doubted Hughes ever saw it.

Note

1. Clint Baxter met and interviewed Big Levine in Las Vegas in April 1994.

5

The Fifties—The Decade of Stress

In 1950, while Mr. Hughes was having all his problems, Jim Haworth had some problems that may be considered small in comparison; however, the frightening trip Iris and he made with their two children in late 1949 was bad enough to make their teeth chatter.

A Short Cut to Always Remember

It was in the fall of 1949. Iris and Jim and their two small children were vacationing in northern Nevada. They were in a little one-horse town called Dinio.

They decided to take a short cut over the mountains to Cedar Ville, California, where a friend they hadn't seen for several years lived.

They got up to Dinio, Nevada, and the service station man told Jim about this mountain road that would save them over one hundred miles, but he said they had better get going, as there was a big snowstorm coming.

The family hadn't gone but about thirty miles on this mountain road when, sure enough, they hit a heavy snowstorm.

They met one truck with a deer hunter in it, but he didn't stop. Shortly after that, the blizzard got worse and Jim's truck gave out on that impassable mountain road. The truck was a '49 Dodge, which Jim had thought was in good shape. So there they were, stranded in the mountains in a bad snowstorm, late at night with no lights, and no hope of anyone coming by till the next spring.

Now, as everyone knows, Jim was no mechanic. He did well to turn the radio on if it was in good shape.

"So what shall we do now?" Iris said. "You shouldn't have ever taken this short cut; now we'll freeze to death."

Jim said "If I had a light I might be able to fix this truck."

"You can't start a fire in this storm. Everything is soaking wet." Iris was getting panicked by then and could see the whole family freezing to death on this lonely mountain road and told Jim so, too.

Well, they stopped arguing and their son, Jerry, and daughter, Rita, thought about a little wooden dollhouse they had in the back of the truck. So Jim got out and smashed the dry dollhouse and with a lot of luck and a book of matches finally got a fire started and built it up with cedar limbs till he had a roaring fire going. He got the kids and Iris out and warmed up. Then Jim could see the truck motor pretty well. He fumbled around with the wiring and discovered the coil wire had jolted off the coil and cut off juice from the motor.

To Iris's surprise, when she turned the key the pickup started.

They were very grateful and Iris knew that someone was watching over them.

Well, they made it to Cedar Ville about 2:00 A.M. and very thankful to get there. Jim has not tried a short cut since.

Hughes in San Limbo

Howard Hughes dreamed and planned his retirement to

his Warm Springs paradise since first sighting it from his D-2 plane. The paranoia of his manic depression after his third near-fatal airplane accident grounded him temporarily from his San Limbo flights. The pain from his fractured leg, his lifelong deafness, and the stress of trying to avoid government and public scrutiny and yet satisfy his executives and thousands of employees were more than his fertile determined mind could bear.

In 1950, Frank Taylor, a wealthy New Yorker, bought the Home Ranch and changed its name to the Warm Springs Ranch. He hired Jim Haworth to manage the ranch, buy cattle, and buy range and water rights. The range rights were in several Nevada counties, but most were in Lincoln County, adjacent to Clark County, Nevada.

In 1950, the U.S. Atomlc Energy Commission designated Frenchman's Flats near Las Vegas as its proving grounds. This worried Howard Hughes to the point of frantically pleading (without success) with top government officials to designate Alaska their choice. Later, in 1953, the commission sponsored a nuclear test at Yucca Flats, Nevada.

Howard Hughes bought 27,000 acres called Husite out of Las Vegas with plans to build a super international airport in a deal with the McCarran Airport.

In November 1950, Howard Hughes, suffering from his third manic depression syndrome, was worried and scared of dying without a will. He had made two former wills and, when feeling better, canceled them. This time, the IRS, as well as the CIA and his executives was demanding financial reports, stock options, etc., which he refused. He spent six months working and reworking the draft of his will, aimed at using his Howard Hughes Medical Research Institute as a nonprofit charity, therefore tax-deductible, while at the same time he wanted to show his concern for public health.

He yearned for love and respect. His lease payments from

his research institute were large enough for him to reap a nice income from his charitable foundation. More than the income, he enjoyed using tax money for his personal charity.

His lifelong concern for his health and fear of contaminants gave him the idea of funding the medical research institution, not a hospital. He named it the Howard Hughes Medical Research Laboratories; it was located in Miami, Florida. The will stated that virtually all of his fortune would go to his research laboratories for scholarships and expenses. After several meetings with his secretary, Nadine Henley, he ordered her to place the will in a safety-deposit box in the First National Bank of Houston and wear the key around her neck. The box was not to be opened until after his death. Copies were made, but not signed.

Howard Hughes became concerned with communism creeping into private enterprise, especially in the movie industry. Although he was not interested in politics for himself and never voted, he was so concerned with the fear of communism in industry that he fired his movie director, Paul Jerrico. He received a commendation from Richard Nixon and the House Un-American Activities Committee and the American Legion for his efforts.

In 1951, he negotiated a deal with Tucson, Arizona, to build the world's largest defense plant for manufacture of his Falcon, the first air-to-air guided missile. Thirty thousand acres were involved. Tucson, at a cost of $459,000, built streets, sewer lines, water line, and a railroad spur, all in anticipation of jobs and taxes. Hughes negotiated for the Defense Department to buy the installation and lease it back to him, eliminating the anticipated taxes expected for Tucson. Hughes had previously hoped to move some of his operations to Nevada because there was no Nevada tax and he wanted to be near his ranch paradise. He also enjoyed the glamour of Las Vegas and the girls available for his movies.

In 1952, Hughes sold RKO to a syndicate. After he sold RKO for $7,345,980, bad publicity caused virtual destruction of RKO. Hughes was forced to take RKO back, retaining the down payment of $1.25 million. He knew he was taking a huge loss but had been temporarily free of the RKO headache when he sold to the syndicate. Now he became embroiled in lawsuits filed by RKO stockholders charging him with self-dealing practices. He contemplated buying them all out and gaining 100 percent control. However, his attention was now more concerned with his rapidly growing Hughes Aircraft Company Electronics (under the supervision of Ramos and Wooldridge). This electronics business's principal customer was the Strategic Air Command.

In 1953–54 he leased a five-room bungalow adjacent to the Desert Inn. He had all the windows taped and sealed and ordered air conditioners installed to eliminate dust and pollen. After he left Las Vegas in 1954, he continued the lease and eventually bought and preserved the house in its original state until his death.

In 1954, he hired a financial expert, Spyros Skouras, to appraise his entire holdings, "preparatory" to selling out. He only wanted to know his worth, not intending to sell.

Hughes Electronics

After the Senate hearings in 1953 Howard Hughes continued losing in Hughes Aircraft. He was urged by long-time business manager Noah Dietrick, still at the home plant (Hughes Tool Company) to rid himself of Hughes Aircraft.

That was against Howard Hughes's principles. He, instead, hired a new team of managers for Hughes Aircraft. The team consisted of two retired air force lieutenant generals, Ora C. Eaker and Howard L. George, and Charles B. Thornton, former Ford Motor Company executive. Their duties were as follows:

- *Eaker*, vice president of Hughes Tool Company, would be liaison between Hughes Tool Company and Hughes Aircraft.
- *George,* vice president and general manager of Hughes Aircraft, was placed in charge of operations.
- *Thornton* was assistant general manager of Hughes Aircraft.

George was credited with building the Air Transport Command from 78 planes to 4,000 planes and 330,000 men. Hughes's first acquaintance with George had been during the filming of *Hell's Angels* in the 1930s. That bit of news was not revealed this time.

The aircraft company was now yielding more profits than the parent Hughes Tool Company, and Dietrick found the executives (George, Thornton, Ramo, Wooldridge) were taking full control of the aircraft division and voiced concern about their authority.

Also, George, Thornton, Ramo, and Wooldridge were concerned about Dietrick's inherent power. They sent two warning memoranda to Hughes asking for a meeting to resolve their differences, stating the aircraft company could not meet its obligations to the air force under the present conditions.

The four aircraft executives met with Hughes. Howard Hughes was not impressed by their urgent complaints, even accusing them as a group, with communistic motives, of plans to take over.

Finally, Ramo and Wooldridge resigned, opened their own plant (the Ramo Wooldridge Corporation), later to become TRW, Inc., and produced more profits than Hughes Aircraft Company.

The security of the air force met with the remaining work force of Hughes Aircraft and urged their giving ninety days' time to deliberate before walking out.

Dietrick fired General George. Thornton resigned and with another executive (Roy M. Ash) founded Litton Industries. Other senior scientists were about to walk out. Assistant secretary of the air force Roger Lewis met with the rest of Hughes Aircraft workers and convinced them to stay the ninety days. Hughes was not afraid of losing the aircraft company. He was used to losing millions on his toys. He was concerned about losing his public image as an aviation genius.

During the upheaval in 1953 at Hughes Aircraft, Hughes found time to tinker with his movie, *The French Line,* starring the voluptuous, provocative Jane Russell, and fight the Motion Picture Producers Association of America, the press, and churches. The bad publicity made the opening night in Saint Louis a roaring success.

In 1953, still another problem confronted Hughes. The demand for more American oil was causing more and more oil wells to be drilled, of course using the Hughes oil drill bit. The Hughes Tool Company was yielding more and more profits, and Hughes was owing the IRS more and more of his income.

Howard Hughes, the industrial giant, was pushed to use his mathematics manipulation to solve the problem. He practiced his own mathematics. In school he had been a poor math student, and he never received a high school diploma. As sole owner of Hughes Tool Company and president of Hughes Aircraft Company, he devised a method to sell Hughes Aircraft Company to a charity. He founded the Howard Hughes Research Institute in Miami, Florida, with the help of Governor Collins in 1956. The institute made lease payments to Hughes Tool Company. Hughes Tool Company profits were poured into the Howard Hughes Research Institute tax-free. The

Howard Hughes Research Institute, with Howard Hughes the only board member, paid Hughes Tool Company (Howard Hughes) the Hughes Aircraft profits in the form of lease payments.

He transferred almost all of his Hughes Aircraft stock into the new Hughes Aircraft Company. The remainder stayed in the old company, now called the Hughes Tool Company, Aircraft Division. Hughes's interest in ranches, land, etc., also included his plan for the Warm Springs (Home) Ranch to be his retirement tax cover.

Initially the IRS turned down the Hughes medical research charity. After extensive IRS hearings, the Howard Hughes Medical Research Institute was accepted as a Hughes Tool Company charitable deduction. Hughes Tool Company donated Hughes Aircraft Company to the Institute. The institute leased the property from Hughes Tool Company, of which Howard Hughes was sole owner. Research and grants were less than the loans and lease payments to Howard Hughes's Hughes Tool Company. The loan to the institute was to be paid off in ten years.

In 1956, an election year, the IRS reconsidered Hughes's tax status because of an unpaid loan of $200,000 by Nixon's brother. Hughes had paid heavily for Nixon's election to vice president. Somehow the IRS, in 1957, granted Hughes tax-exempt status for HHMRI. He selected Miami for the institute.

Howard Hughes used his tax savings to invest in air force contracts, TWA, and other holdings and left the HHMRI in all his wills to receive the bulk of his estate.

Fearful of germs and his health, he demanded imported water, sealed off his bedroom, fought nuclear testing in Nevada, and had bizarre diets. One time 220 gallons of banana ice cream were made for him. Two days after enjoying his first meal of the banana ice cream, he said it was time to change back to vanilla. He surveyed the state of Nevada to determine a source of pure water. He discovered that the warm springs of the Home Ranch would be ideal for his future health.

In 1954, during the IRS and HHMRI episode, another sharp thorn was driven into Howard Hughes's psyche. He learned that Jean Peters, his onetime girlfriend, was dating another man, whom he feared was a government agent. Howard had, seven years before, given Jean Peters a diamond and sapphire ring but wanted to wait to marry her. (Howard's wise personal habit was never to hurry in any important decision.)

Howard hired two top Washington lawyers, in the firm of Hogan and Hartson, to investigate Jean Peters's romancing with Stewart W. Cramer III and feared a conspiracy to undo his HHMRI tax-exempt-status application. At Hughes's request, Hogan and Hartson retained Robert Aimee Maheu, a former FBI agent, to investigate Jean Peters's affair. This was Maheu's first dealing with Howard Hughes. Robert Aimee Maheu was later to be the most important person in Howard Hughes's life.

Robert Aimee Maheu was born in Waterville, Maine. Bob Maheu now states that "one thing says more about me than all the other pictures and plaques combined, a sign that reads: ELM CITY BOTTLING. Elm City Bottling was a small carbonated beverage company that my father ran from a barn behind his grocery store in Waterville, Maine."

Bob attended Holy Cross College in Worcester, Massachusetts, where he worked his way through law school waiting tables.

There he met one of his closest friends, named Edward Bennett Williams, the man who later introduced him to Howard Hughes. After graduation from college, Bob joined the FBI as a special agent. He was active in many political maneuvers for the FBI and CIA and formed his own company, Robert A. Maheu & Associates.

Robert Maheu had some very nervous moments and sleepless nights while investigating people such as Nixon and Onassis and others abroad during the Second World War. When contacted to work for the fabulous Howard Hughes, the richest man in the United States, Maheu said he would contract with him but not be an employee. Of course time would tell.

Robert Maheu did not know the identity of his client (Howard Hughes) and at the time, in need of the assignment, had no idea it would lead to his fabled new life from then until Hughes's death as a paranoid drug addict.

Robert Maheu now lives with his wife, Yvette, in Las Vegas.

In February 1956, Hughes finally ordered a fleet of jets for TWA. He filed with the CAB to build his own jets in Florida and sell them to TWA. This caper was never accomplished. At this point Howard Hughes contacted his boyhood friend Dudley Sharp, who was now assistant secretary of the air force, for advice—advice that was never accepted.

On January 12, 1957, soon after Jean Peters divorced Stuart W. Cramer III, Howard Hughes with four aides met Jean Peters in an upstairs room of a second-rate Tonopah, Nevada, motel where they were married under the assumed names of G. A. Johnson (for Hughes) and Marion Evans (for Jean Peters).

Howard's standby Lockheed Constellation took them back to Los Angeles. All was accomplished in one day.

During 1957, Hughes lived in the Bahamas and was involved in a big land deal. It failed and he flew home to Los Angeles alone. At this time he insisted on Robert Maheu being his only spokesperson. Maheu dropped all his other business and went to Washington to try to delay nuclear testing in Nevada.

TWA became more and more in debt with Howard Hughes's various changes in management. June 23, 1960,

TWA president Charles S. Thomas resigned. TWA was forced into a voters' trust by its financiers.

After Thomas, with no stock options, resigned, he became manager of ranch development for the huge Irvine Corporation in Southern California.

In 1959, Howard Hughes hired Maheu to leave his business, move to Hollywood, and become his alter ego. Greg Boutzer, Hughes's attorney, arranged for the move.

During 1959, in the middle of the TWA problem, Howard Hughes ordered Maheu to hire the most beautiful Miss America contestants for a film he never produced. Then Maheu arranged for and shipped Howard Hughes by train to Boston, where he stayed a short time.

The big event of 1959 was when Hughes's fear of communism caused him to order Robert Maheu to work with the CIA to arrange for the assassination of Fidel Castro in Cuba. Maheu met with Nevada gangsters and formulated a plan. The failed invasion of Cuba prevented the plan's activation.

6
Hughes and TWA

After 1959, there were no more movies for Howard Hughes. He enjoyed seeing them on his television screen in his bedroom, that's all.

The biggest nightmare of his life was during those six years (1960–1966) fighting the lenders of Wall Street, the IRS, and his TWA stockholders. Trying to be number one in the airlines, he invested millions of his own money as well as what he could borrow. He cost Convair $490 million in contracted unaccepted aircraft—more than Ford lost on its Edsel automobile.

It was six years of litigation and headaches. He fired or lost several presidents of TWA, until Charles C. Tillinghast brought the airline well into the black.

Disgruntled stockholders forced Hughes to place his shares into trust and finally sell out. This was the greatest stroke of luck in Howard Hughes's career. In 1966, he sold his 78 percent of TWA shares for $86 per share, a profit of $546,540,000, over one-half billion dollars, the biggest single check ever received by an individual in a business transaction.

During the early sixties Jim Haworth was busy working the Warm Springs Ranch for Francis Taylor and himself.

In 1966 that same year, after the half-billion-dollar windfall, Howard Hughes took the half-billion dollars and took a train to Boston.

Hughes was advised to leave California to avoid the IRS investigators and spies into his finances. He decided to go to Boston by train, not by plane.

In late 1966, Thanksgiving Day, Howard Hughes decided Boston was not for him. He ordered Robert Maheu to arrange a train back to Las Vegas and arrange for his accommodations on the top floor of his Desert Inn.

After Boston, on November 27, 1966, Howard Hughes insisted that Robert Maheu take over, going to Las Vegas as Hughes's advance man and handling all Hughes's affairs in Las Vegas. Hughes made himself a promise to stop running and buy the Warm Springs Ranch. He also had his eye on buying the best Las Vegas hotels and casinos. He was vitally concerned about a report by Dr. Allan Ryan that a nuclear test near Las Vegas would probably cause an earthquake.

At present there were three most urgent plans in the mind of the man of San Limbo: (1) He must prevent nuclear testing in the Nevada Desert. (2) He must buy all the desert property he could find. He was afraid the nuclear testing would cause an earthquake and destroy his Nevada operations. The beautiful, huge Warm Springs Ranch and ranges would provide a safe retirement haven for him and for his wife, Jean Peters. (3) He must exterminate the gangster influence in Las Vegas and buy up the hotel-casinos run by hoodlums.

Jean Peters was through with the uncertainty of Hughes's offer of a permanent home on the Warm Springs Ranch. She refused to go back to Las Vegas with Howard. She never saw him again. Disappointed and stressed, he indulged more heavily in drugs and sealed himself in his bedroom penthouse.

Through Richard Gray's legal persuasion, the Nevada Gaming Commission and the Clark County Gaming Board granted Howard Hughes permits to own and operate Las Vegas casinos and hotels, a total of seven, plus his already valuable land obtained along the Strip in Las Vegas after the El Rancho Vegas burned.

Howard Hughes became Nevada's biggest gambler, surpassing William Harrah, all by a man who did not gamble. He vowed he would make it exciting and fun for the eager public, without cheating. Even the U.S. Justice Department could not stop Hugh Howard Hughes now.

Howard Hughes's worst competitor was Kirk Kerkorian, an eighth-grade-dropout automobile salesman who became a millionaire through military air transport contracts.

Kerkorian had learned to fly at an early age. In 1941 he obtained a commercial pilot's license and bought a C-47 and started the Los Angeles Air Service. During the Korean War he obtained lucrative military contracts and was plummeted into a major international air carrier renamed Trans International Air Lines.

Kerkorian came to Las Vegas in 1967 with a $100 million fortune. He bought Bugsy Siegel's Flamingo Hotel and Casino. The Flamingo was a loser that Kerkorian had visions of developing into the biggest high-rise hotel in Las Vegas, to be called the International.

Howard Hughes was already planning to build the biggest, tallest hotel in Las Vegas. He tried to deter Kerkorian's going ahead with the International by having Robert Maheu tell Kerkorian that Hughes's Sands project was not going ahead because of Hughes's knowledge that the Atomic Energy Commission was going to do underground tests nearby and that independent tests had shown a likelihood of a Las Vegas earthquake. It was well known that Hughes had pulled all possible strings in Washington to prevent these tests.

It was learned by Clint Baxter from "Big Levine," a former bell captain at the old Flamingo, that Howard Hughes earlier had leased the penthouse of the old Flamingo as a haven for many of his RKO actresses. Big told of his twenty-four-hour waiting on Howard Hughes as personal bell captain of the hotel. One of his duties was arranging for Hughes to take over the dining room each morning for buffet breakfasts for Hughes's girls.

Through 1968 to 1970 Howard Hughes met with the drastic reality of possible bankruptcy. He was first confronted with the increasing drastic losses from his frantic acquisitions. He was in his worst financial condition at the beginning of 1967, even though Hughes Tool Company had $607.7 million in the bank in the form of cash and U.S. Government securities.

In the meantime, Howard Hughes was investing in his wild purchases of many nonfunctioning gold mines in Nevada and the purchase of the Warm Springs Ranch.

As if this were not enough strain on his rapidly depleting funds, his hotels and casinos showed huge losses; the McCarran Airport operation was losing money, as was his Alamo Airlines. His new executive, Bill Gay, claimed the Warm Springs Ranch for himself and stated that the ranch was a losing white elephant.

On top of it all, the country was faced with a devastating depression.

Howard Hughes was rapidly sliding into a state of physical and mental collapse. He added to his stress with finagling a buyout of the failing Air West Airlines. He was spending $367,579 per day, and by 1969 Howard Hughes was deep in debt.

Howard Hughes's Wild Investments

From 1960 through 1969, Hughes, among his other interests, was embroiled in obtaining a contract from the navy

Self-portrait of Jim Haworth, Howard Hughes's man.

for light helicopters. He finally delivered some of the contracted planes at a loss of $90 million.

Richard Gray, Hughes Tool Company lawyer, was summoned to Las Vegas to close the Desert Inn deal and was only supposed to stay in Las Vegas two or three weeks, but ended up staying and managing Hughes's acquisitions and enjoying Hughes Warm Springs Ranch for three years. Howard Hughes was intent on land purchases and ranches and owning a million-acre land empire.

Howard Hughes, becoming disenchanted with aircraft design and manufacture, was losing some of his vigor and even refused to ride in airplanes. He stayed confined to his sealed Desert Inn bedroom suite on top of the Desert Inn Hotel. His first ranch purchase was that of the Madam Krupp Spring Mountain Ranch near Las Vegas. It belonged to Vera Krupp, wealthy wife of Alfred Krupp, of the Krupp Munitions empire in Germany.

During 1966–68, Dick Gray was principal legal adviser, although ignored by Hughes in his frantic purchase of six Las Vegas hotels and casinos. During this time, Howard Hughes proclaimed Robert Maheu his man, his alter ego. Robert Maheu appointed himself president of Hughes's Nevada operations. Although Hughes Tool Company in Houston owned the Nevada operations, Maheu did the wheeling and dealing for Howard Hughes and for himself. Maheu built himself a beautiful home, reconditioned his yacht, the *Aloette*, built himself a mountain "cabin" (he called it a chalet), and arranged for niceties for his son Peter and friends all to the tune of millions of dollars, besides his handsome yearly pay of one half-million dollars, plus expenses and extravagances. Most of the extravagances were paid by the Frontier Hotel, which belonged to Hughes. In fact, Hughes encouraged Maheu's excesses for his own ego. Robert Maheu made the Frontier Hotel executive suite his office for Nevada operations.

Dick Gray was emerging as the most sincere of Howard Hughes's managers. He helped in legal ways to obtain purchases and gambling rights even though he advised Howard Hughes against involvement. He did not press for stock options or use his authority to "use" Howard Hughes.

Dick Gray, Hughes's Houston lawyer, knew Hughes's longing for land, ranches, and animals and advised Howard to lay off acquisition of further hotels and, instead, invest in comfortable land holdings. Dick Gray was the only Hughes executor with a profound interest in natural land and what it contained. With his experience and advice, Dick Gray proposed and finalized the purchase of the Krupp Ranch while Hughes was becoming worried over his overexpansion in hotels and his rapidly diminishing Las Vegas income.

Nevertheless, his biggest dream was coming true, the purchase of the Warm Springs, Nevada, ranch. This fitted well with Howard's lifelong dream of owning most of Nevada, with lots of cattle and horses and, above all, his controlled, pure environment with no more worries about water purity, air purity, and land free from nuclear tests.

After the purchase of the Warm Springs Ranch, Howard Hughes had hoped to entice his wife, Jean Peters, to live with him there. However, she refused to come back to Las Vegas from their Boston trip. Although she still loved him and knew he loved her, she, like Howard's first wife, Ella, could no longer stand in a corner while Howard went on his bizarre San Limbo trips. She had enjoyed their short stay in rural Rancho Santa Fe, California. She did not know of Howard's longtime plan to buy the Warm Springs Ranch, else she might have stayed with him.

The 1967–68 Mad Buying Spree That Nearly Broke the Once Billionaire

Throughout the year 1967 and into 1968, Hughes had been spending money at the rate of $367,579 a day. By December 31, 1968, Hughes would run through $268.7 million.[1] He bought Nevada hotels, casinos, gold and silver mines, land, airlines, and airports and was heavily involved in state and federal government "investments" to promote his ego desires.

Most of his 1967–68 investments were unprofitable, resulting in huge losses and lawsuits. The realization that he had squandered his fortune caused him to sink into his final manic depression, remaining in his bed with his ready supply of drugs provided by his attendants and executives escaping Maheu's watchful eye.

During this time Hughes secretly instructed his trusted executive Dick Gray to seek out the owner of Warm Springs Ranch and negotiate the ranch purchase by R. W. Webb for Hughes Tool Company of Houston.

Little attention was paid by Maheu or Hughes's other executives to the ranch operations. They were involved in the purchase of gold mines for Hughes. Mention is made on page 367 of Donald L. Bartlett and James B. Steele's *Empire: The Life, Legend and Madness of Howard Hughes* as follows: "His Castaways Hotel and Casino consistently lost money, as did the Frontier Hotel and Casino. His fixed based operations at McCarran Airport and Alamo Airlines were unprofitable. So was his Warm Springs Ranch."[2]

Howard Hughes's First Ranch, the Madam Krupp Ranch

In 1968 Howard Hughes negotiated the purchase of the 518-acre Madam Krupp Ranch at Mount Charleston near Las Vegas. This Spring Mountain ranch was named the Madam Krupp Ranch by Hughes's executives. Hughes also bought the Riddle estate in the exclusive area of Las Vegas.

Howard bought these two magnificent properties, along with his later purchase of all the Warm Springs desert property, with hopes of Jean Peters returning from Boston and living in one of them. He wrote to Jean and called her several times extolling the plans he had for the ranch with its own landing strip, luxury home, and a stable of horses and a herd of cattle. He would move his office there. (He had never had an office. His office was any handy telephone booth.) Jean was interested only if Howard lived there, too. This Howard would not commit to. He would stay in his Desert Inn penthouse.

After Hughes purchased the ranch, Vera Krupp continued to live there for a short time with her cowboys and cattle.

The Indian Burial as Related by Jim Haworth

Howard Hughes hired Jim Haworth to manage and work the ranch. Jim's first job on the Madam Krupp Ranch was gathering wild range cattle from a mesa between the ranch and Lake Mead and moving them up to the ranch. Jim related how he and two cowboys, Dave and Newt Bundy, drove the cattle to the sandbars along the Virgin River. They roped and tied about forty head of wild cows. They moved all the cattle they could out of the heavy brush and drove them around the mesa point and up the valley. Jim states, "We hauled and worked with them for probably a week before we got them out of there and we didn't even get thanks from Madam Krupp.

"One day Dave, Newt and I were asked to help Madam's cowboys bury an Indian in a grave they had dug up on a hill on the Krupp ranch. When we got there, the coffin with the Indian was still at the bottom of the hill. We had to wrestle that coffin up the hill. The Indian, Buster Wilson, was born and raised on the ranch. Buster Wilson's father sold the ranch to Madam Krupp. Buster lived alone in a little cabin at Roberts Spring on Mount Charleston. He didn't work for Madam Krupp. Anyway, old Buster died and they had him in a casket when I got up there and so we were all ready to start carrying him up this damn hill. About that time here came a whole load of hippies and they were drunk. They had come to Buster's funeral. They had been buddies with Buster on the mountain, so they got more than the rest of the pallbearers. We didn't like it much. There was that damn hill and the casket staring us in the face, so they had to sit down on Buster's coffin and have a big drink of whiskey before they started up the hill. Just about every fifty feet or so, they would have to stop and have another drink of whiskey. Then they'd get their guitars out and sing to old Buster. They made it up the hill and they opened the casket and sang a few more tunes and had a few more drinks of whiskey. They had another full bottle so they poked it down in old Buster's bag in the coffin, so he wouldn't get thirsty."

Newt Bundy worked for Madam Krupp. She used to ride with the cowboys gathering cattle. Newt said that when it was pretty hot out there in the summer and they came to a water trough, she pulled off all her clothes and jumped in right in front of the cowboys. Newt said they didn't mind at all.

Madam Krupp used to help gather the cattle and rode right with the cowboys. When she went riding with the cowboys, she gave her jewelry to Newt Bundy to hold. He shoved a big diamond ring and other jewelry in his chaps. Some time after they got back to the ranch, she asked where the diamonds were. Newt said, "Hell, they are probably down there in the chaps pocket in the saddle room, been hanging up down there a week."

Later she sold the ring to Elizabeth Taylor for $30,000.

One night there was a robbery at the Krupp mansion. Madam Krupp had a boyfriend named Hal Bruderston. When the thieves broke in, Hal and Madam Krupp were in the living room. As Jim says, "They rolled them two up in a rug and left them. They were found the next morning when the maid came to work."

On March 22, 1967, Howard Hughes bought the Desert Inn for $13,200,000 from Moe Dalitz. Moe, former member of the Mayfield Road Gang in Cleveland, had tried to force Hughes to vacate his rented top floor. Howard refused to leave. He ordered Maheu to buy the damn place.

Bob Maheu hired Gen. Gene Nigro as property agent. Later, Hughes bought the Warm Springs Ranch.

Richard Gray (Hughes's Houston attorney from the Hughes Tool Company) was summoned to Las Vegas to handle the real estate purchases and the gaming permits from the Nevada Gaming Board.

On July 1, 1967, Howard Hughes bought the Sands Hotel for $14.6 million.

Also during that year, casino fever continued with Hughes. He bought the Frontier, Castaways, Silver Slipper, and Landmark Towers. Robert Maheu and Richard Gray arranged the casino management contracts.

In 1968, the glitter of gold was in the eyes of Howard Hughes and especially in the eyes of some of his executives. The first purchase was the Goodsprings (Hill Property) mine for $240,000.

Other mines and so-called gravel pits were purchased for Hughes by certain executives and resold at huge profits.

Notes

1. Donald L. Bartlett and James B. Steele, *Empire: The Life, Legend and Madness of Howard Hughes* (New York: W. W. Norton Company 1979), pp. 366–67.
2. Ibid.

7

Gold Butte

This story by Chuck Voglewede is of his experiences while working with Newt Bundy for Jim Haworth and Howard Hughes.

What have I been doing wrong? I thought as I rode into Gunlock, Utah, a town too small for a saloon. *I should be in Wyoming by now.* I had spent forty-four days in the saddle and covered barely three hundred miles, which figures to about seven miles a day. For a week I had been doubting my horse's endurance; the dark bay gelding was getting thin. Gunlock, that's where I hooked up with a fellow named Newt Bundy.

Newt had a grizzled, saddle-worn look and he moved in a slow, bent manner, like someone who just had a hard day on a green colt. Newt pointed to the pasture in his backyard, and I turned my gelding loose there. After unfolding a couple of beat-up wooden chairs, Newt and I sat under a shade tree and got acquainted.

I told Newt how far I'd come, where I was going, and asked if he knew of any horses for sale. He was busy lighting up a cigarette, but after shaking the match ten or fifteen times and taking a few draws of smoke, he replied, "Yeah, maybe."

Melted into that splintered chair, Newt looked about fifty years old; his two-day beard was mostly white, his face was deeply tanned and weathered, and the corners of his eyes creased as he sat studying the slow movements of my horse. I sat and said nothing and looked at the horse, too.

Five minutes crawled by and finally I said, "Maybe I can get a riding job around here, give this horse a rest, and then head out again."

Newt lit another Marlboro, inhaled, and through the smoke drawled, "If'n I was you, I'd sell that hoss and buy a ticket for a Greyhound bus."

But I was determined to finish my ride and Newt seemed to understand, becoming less reticent as the sky darkened. With a telephone call he lined up a job for both of us. The next morning, long before first light, we tossed our saddles and bedrolls into Newt's old pickup, waved good-bye to his wife, and then headed for a place called Gold Butte.

Gold Butte was a sculpture of rocks somewhere in the high desert bordering Lake Mead, Nevada. Raising a plume of dust, we drove through hills scattered with yucca, mesquite, and burrobrush to the cow camp. There were two gutted shacks, a camper trailer, and a corral full of horses. Over a cup of the strongest coffee I had ever tasted, I met five other riders.

Jimmy Haworth, the cow boss, was older than Newt and had silver-gray hair and a peppery mustache. He was a small, quiet man with bowed legs and a twinkle in his eye. When Jimmy talked, we listened.

Then there was Big Jim, six-foot-four and full of muscle. He demanded a good deal of respect in the camp; not so much on account of his size or his ability to shoe horses, but because Big Jim was the cook. He could also handle a rope.

But the roping honors went to Fernando, the thirty-year-old Mexican. He couldn't speak much English but could make a rope sing.

Tom Tom was a twenty-five-year-old Paiute Indian who rode a paint pony called Broken Arrow or Crooked River or whatever Tom Tom felt like calling it at the time.

The last was Whitmore, a burly bearded fellow who lived alone somewhere in the desert. He had the habit of emitting low warning groans while he ate. Whitmore did the truck driving, hauling calves to market or giving our horses a lift to some remote corner of the range.

By range, I mean open range; 400,000 acres of sandy, rolling hills and deep rocky canyons, a hiding place for 800 head of skittish cattle. Other than a few wooden corrals, there were no fences.

That first day, we gathered the cattle nearest to camp. They were mostly Brahma, and if they saw you first, it took some hard riding to get them stopped. I rode a tall Appaloosa whose ribs were as obvious as the frame of a derelict shipwreck, a horse that had been running loose on the range all winter. We put in a good thirty miles, usually at a bone-jarring jog, and at the end of the day that rangy Appaloosa was still plenty rambunctious—I was not. After a single helping of supper, I rolled my blanket out under the stars and collapsed into a deep sleep.

The next day, riding single file through a maze of canyons, we followed the cow boss to a different area. He had his eyes on the ground, tracking. Occasionally I saw Tom Tom on a hill off in the distance, scouting for cattle. We hunted and gathered, and by and by we had a small herd under control.

Later, as we pushed them toward the corral, some of the wiser animals broke herd. While I remained at drag, the other riders shagged in all directions, ropes twirling and hooves pounding the ground. When the dust settled, most of the original bunch were corralled.

One time when this happened, I shook out a loop and joined in the chase. Had I known that unbranded stock was first priority, I wouldn't have chased that old cow into the hills and gotten myself lost. Sometime after dark I wandered into camp to a cold meal. The fire was burning low and the silent faces I met were visible only when cigarettes glowed. To the boss I said, "I musta taken the wrong trail, at the wrong place, at the wrong time."

I learned that the man who blunders is sentenced to ground work. The next morning Jimmy said, "We only need six riders today, so why don't you stay here and collect firewood." And collect firewood I did. All day I chopped and piled every scrap I could find. Jimmy seemed pleased with my work, as I was allowed to ride the following day.

I stayed close to Jimmy and Newt after that, realizing that I didn't know a hell of a lot about the country, the cattle, or wrangling in general. Both men had spent their lives working from a horse, and through them I could see glimpses of life a hundred years ago. Fernando taught me some rope catches, heeling, forefooting, pitches, slips, and the Hoolihan or backhand. And I learned from Big Jim, who took me aside one day and said I wasn't eating enough. His huge hand gripping my neck convinced me that I should indeed eat more.

The branding system worked better than a well-oiled machine. Five of us suffered afoot while Jimmy and Fernando sat horseback. Ground workers paired up while Newt kept the irons hot and branded the animals we held down. Thick yellow smoke and dust hung in the air and severed parts from castrating sizzled at the fire's edge—our lunch.

We worked as fast as possible, not relishing the ground work. With a single throw of a loop, Fernando consistently heeled two or three head, which made double or triple work for us. We could average a calf per minute that way, much faster than a squeeze chute allowed. But it was tough work and the burns, scratches, and kicked shins were not too soon forgotten.

For three weeks I rode, roped, and learned much about working cattle. The days were long, the nights short, and the coffee was strong. My only clothes were torn and bloodstained; my face was unshaven.

The weekends were a relief. While the others went home, I tended horses, bathed in the water trough, and roamed the hills looking for old mine shafts. I came across a couple of tombstones one day. Buried in one grave was William Garret, an outlaw who had spent his last days in seclusion at Gold Butte. William was the less famous brother of Pat Garret, the man who killed Billy the Kid.

There was a lot of history embedded in Gold Butte. The ranch had been owned by the Mormon church and, before that, by billionaire Howard Hughes. It had also been owned by a German steel heiress who liked to ride along on the roundups. In those days Newt was the cow boss and he carried the Madam's jewels while she rode. He once carried over a million dollars' worth of broaches and rings into those hills. Later, when the madam asked Newt where her jewels were, he replied, "Well, I reckon they're down to the barn in my chaps pocket." She was so impressed with the unlikeliness of being robbed that she often asked Newt to escort her on trips so that he could carry the jewels. (So Newt said.)

It was fortunate that I could cook a little, because Big Jim departed after the first week and I inherited his job. It was a promotion from dishwasher but meant nothing but extra work. After a long day, I had to feed six hungry men and then had to roll out early to fix breakfast. I learned how to make their taste of coffee. Whitmore said he liked his strong enough to float a horseshoe.

One morning as I was gathering kindling, Tom Tom woke and said, "What are you doing?"

"Building a fire," I said. "Isn't this how you Indians do it?"

"Hell, no. Indians do it easier than that. Watch."

Tom Tom tossed a few heavy branches into the fire pit and poured a half-gallon of gasoline on. The ensuing explosiion lit up the predawn darkness, and coffee was done early that morning.

One evening I found that Newt, on his last supply run, had bought cracked wheat instead of flour.

"I can't make gravy with this," I said.

"Sure you can," the old duffers egged me on. "You're a good enough cook."

So I tried. The gravy turned out more like wet bread, and the crew avoided it like they would a sidewinder. I showed them how delicious it was by eating three helpings.

The next day I had chills even though the temperature was over a hundred degrees. I was sick but managed to stay in the saddle until we returned to camp. Shivering in my bedroll, I heard someone say, "Find him a pill; he don't look so good." Fernando came up with a dirty unidentified tablet and offered it to me. I declined.

Then Jimmy said, "Hell, you're just all bound up from eating that lousy gravy. Drink a cup of Wesson oil; that'll cure ya."

So I drank it, and it cured me.

One night Newt took over as cook and decided to make his famous biscuits. After mixing the dough, he greased and filled one of the three Dutch ovens. He stirred up the coals, put the oven on, and covered the lid with hot embers. Then he sat back and bragged on his cooking while the biscuits baked. Ten minutes later he removed the lid and the Dutch oven was empty!

"Now where'd them things run off ta?" he pondered aloud. He tipped back his old Stetson, scratched his forehead, and looked around the camp. Then, with the toe of his boot, he flipped the lids off the other two ovens and there were his biscuits, still cold. Laughter echoed into the night.

Western humor is spontaneous but can also be shrewd. At least once a day I was reminded of a racy town down by the lake: "If those cattle are on the shoreline, we might be moving 'em back right through Copper City," or, "The last time I was to Copper City they had five new dancin' girls, and mighty pretty fillies at that!"

On Friday before my last weekend, Jimmy looked me in the eyes as he prepared to leave and warned, "Now don't you be runnin' off ta Copper City and gettin' all drunked up, ya hear?"

Tom Tom hung around until Saturday morning, and I asked him where exactly Copper City was.

"Follow Garret Canyon down to the lake and then go south about five miles. You can't miss it."

I grabbed my saddlebags, walked down to the corral, and started saddling Jimmy's best horse. I was mounted and ready to go when I heard Tom Tom laughing.

"What are you laughing about? Are those the right directions?" I asked.

"Oh they're the right directions all right," he said, "but I can't let you go. Copper City died when the dancin' girls left. There ain't nothin' there now!"

I had swallowed hook, line, and sinker.

Three weeks of riding hard and fighting Brahmas toughened me mentally and physically. I was in riding shape and prepared to continue my journey to North Dakota. When all the cattle were gathered and branded, Newt and I returned to Utah.

One look at that poor horse of mine, though, and I knew he couldn't go 1,500 miles. He hadn't gained enough weight. Newt said the horse just wouldn't graze; he was a city horse, born and raised in a stall and fed by hand. What I needed was a good, strong desert horse.

Newt had to fetch a horse back in Nevada, so we hauled my "give-out" city horse along to Jimmy Haworth's ranch. I traded all my wages and my horse for that derelict Appaloosa, whose ribs had disappeared under flesh and muscle during all those thirty- and forty-mile jaunts.

Just before I left Newt Bundy's place in Gunlock, he said to me, "All the time yer a-ridin' an' sore an' chokin' on dust, mile after mile, you jist keep thinkin' 'bout poor Newt."

I was on my way again.

8

The Gold Mines

During 1966 and 1967, Howard Hughes, itchy for further Nevada control, thereby increasing his billionaire fortune, ordered his executives to locate and buy all the abandoned gold mines and claims in Nevada. He was living up to his stated tremendous interest in nature, the Earth, and its hidden minerals. Howard Hughes hired John Meir to buy the mines.

By early 1969, Howard Hughes held title to some seven hundred claims involving 14,000 acres and had spent $10.5 million acquiring them. Most of the land and mine claims were bought and resold by Bill Gay and Hughes's Mormon aides without Hughes's knowledge—a neat scam of their own. Jack Cleveland did most of the dealing with Meir, without Hughes's knowledge. Also, Meir was part owner of Cleveland's Basic Industries Business.

Lorin Bunker, retired chief of police of Las Vegas, was hired by Hughes to straighten out the mine situation as well as supervise Hughes's security agents. In 1967 Hughes sent Bunker to establish his office in the Tonopah, Nevada, mining area, as mine accountant. With his mining experience, Lorin rapidly discovered the conspiracy and waste of millions in unwarranted purchases.

After Lorin Bunker's investigation into the mining ventures, he was relieved of his status as supervisor of security by Bill Gay. The mining operation was defunct. With no respect for Lorin Bunker's efforts (of course), Lorin was relegated to work on the Warm Springs Ranch under Jim Haworth. Jim had no proper place for Lorin, so he sent him to operate the Conaway Ranch (often called the Caliente Ranch), which Jim had just bought for Howard Hughes. Lorin was alone on the Conaway Ranch for two or three months.

Lorin Bunker wrote several letters and reports indicating his displeasure in the mining management. In 1991 these communications were presented by Lorin to Jim Haworth and Clint Baxter to be included in this book. Lorin Bunker was well aware of the improprieties of John Meir, who was hired by Bill Gay to be in charge of the mining operations.

Lorin Bunker is a faithful Mormon, as are Jim Haworth and Iris Haworth.

Howard Hughes hired Bunker to be head of security for Nevada operations. After retirement, he made his permanent home in Overton, Nevada, and he lives there yet, not far from the Warm Springs Ranch. Some of his stories and excerpts are on the following pages.

My Experience with the Gold Mines
by Lorin Bunker

Tonopah, Goldfield, Manhattan, and many other mining districts enjoyed a surge of excitement when the rumor came that Howard Hughes was turning his vast wealth into the mining industry. Many an old-timer said that mines were depleted and if there was any commercial ore left, it would be too expensive to reopen the mines. However, there were many hopefuls whose judgment was based on wishful thinking. Nevertheless, they were all in agreement that the Hughes empire could conquer where all else had failed.

As I completed an assignment at the Landmark Hotel,

Jack Hooper called me to his office and asked if I would help the company in locating some mining property that they had never seen. I agreed to do so, and it was a pleasant and exciting assignment. Through unworthy and greedy employers and some sharpshooters in the mining industry, Hughes bought about 18 million dollars' worth of mining property consisting of about 3,000 claims, with only about 250 of them being patented, the same being dug out or never having much valuable ore to start with.

I don't know how many millions were spent in drilling holes, surveying, and geological reports. Someplace there are voluminous files that tell of that which was done.

There were those in the Hughes organization and those of the mining world that took options on the properties and got control of the properties and sold them for a fabulous amount.

With some of the deals the negotiators told the claim owners to go out and stake more claims and that it was necessary to show that it was a large project. So gravel pits were salted with mineralized ore to show their potential worth.

Some properties were just gravel pits from isolated claims that had been patented in years gone by.

Others showed the struggle of a poor man trying to develop his dream. These kinds of people received little for their labors, but as one such individual said, "They sure made a profit over what they gave me."

Among those involved in the mining world were promoters, politicians, the mining division of the state, and others. One promoter, after making several million, deserted his friend and went to Canada. Another associated with the state mining division took his money and hid it, as he didn't trust the banks. Probably there are prospectors still looking for his cache of hidden money.

Manhattan was practically a ghost town, but Hughes

spent a large sum of money in drilling and developing the area for a leach process to recover the ore. When the project started mining, an engineer from the U.S. Bureau of Mines claimed he was experienced in this process and came and offered his expertise. The local Hughes managers turned him down, perhaps they did not want to be overshadowed with so much professional knowledge.

Nevertheless, they let me have a company vehicle and I got a series of maps of the separate area and went searching for the mining claims that Hughes had purchased. I took a grub box and a bedroll, as I did not intend to get hung up in some faraway place. Then, too, I did not intend to live out of hotels and restaurants and run up a bill for my services. As I found all the claims and put them on my own map I made a chart and report on the claims as to what I thought of their possibilities.

While I was showing a noted visiting geologist some of the Hughes claims in Tonopah he said that north of the highway going to Ely there never had been any ore bodies found. Knowing that Hughes had options on several claims in that area with a price tag of over one half-million dollars, I felt obligated to make a call to Bill Gay, the head honcho in the California office. I went through the special phone number that I had, and no one knew me and they would not take the call. Their security was so tight that they had shut themselves away from the world. Nevertheless, I did get the information to them not to pick up the options on those claims. That was quite a savings to them, for which I never ever received a thanks.

I met an interesting couple living in the twilight years of their lives. They had a little cabin among the cedars in Manhattan. As I visited with them and took note of their humble circumstances I had nothing but admiration for them. On the stand near where I sat I saw a catalog with supplies for dogs, the vitamins, pills, etc., for the general health of these animals. I asked about their dog and they said they didn't have one.

Being curious, I asked what need they had for their catalog of penicillin and supplies for these animals.

They answered that in their research they found that many of the things listed therein were practically the same things that doctors prescribed for humans, and at a much lower price. The figured, *The items are more in our price range and we are in good health, so why not use them?*

There is no doubt that we as humans were ripped off even as Hughes was being ripped off.

There was another old fellow living out his life on his claims. He had traveled far and near but enjoyed the solitude of the mining claims. While I was there, a party that was interested in acquiring his claim came to see him.

They negotiated back and forth, agreeing on the price and value of the claims. The negotiating ended when the people wanting the property asked, "Can I pay for it in yearly payments?"

The answer was quick in coming: "There are no time payments. I am ninety-eight years old and I want to enjoy it now, not tomorrow."

The Hughes empire spent thousands of dollars in buying posts and wire and chain-link fencing to enclose their claims at Tonopah. The fending was never put up. I contacted Jim Haworth over at the ranching division and told him of this wire, and he got a lot of it to fence some of the ranching property. He also got a diesel truck that the company had bought.

Around some of the mining shafts there were usually some outdoor toilets. They were from three- to five-holers in a lumber shack put over a pit. The purpose was to relieve the miners before going down into the mines to work. After all the years when no labor was performed in the mines or in the toilets, there were those who came to clean out the toilet. They were looking for old whiskey bottles that could well be collector's items.

Fred Steen, an old company bookkeeper, told me where some of the ore was piled that probably was milling ore from the Belmont. The powers that be were not interested and they never sampled the same in the fancy assay office they built.

My sojourn with the mining division of the Hughes Company was most interesting. I left with clean hands and a pure heart. I saved them thousands of dollars more than the small wages I received.

Money Saved Is Money Earned
by Lorin Bunker

There was a time when the buyers and sellers of mining claims were working on the Hughes empire like Mr. Hughes owned Fort Knox. The powers that be were burning with the buying fever.

There was a group of claims in the Tonopah area that were in escrow to the empire for a half-million dollars. A noted geologist came by and accidentally said that these claims had never proven to be of any worth.

I happened to push the right button, and the Hughes empire never took these claims out of escrow. There is an old saying: "Money saved is money earned."

I never did receive any thanks, but of course, one shouldn't expect a thanks on top of one's wages.

Too Smart to Learn
by Lorin Bunker

Manhattan was on the verge of becoming a ghost town. In fact, the ghosts were waiting to take over the town, but a few stouthearted natives refused to leave. The lure of gold was still strong, and when Mr. Hughes's stalwarts bought heavily in the camp, the hopes of the natives soared.

The empire spent plenty of money surveying, drilling holes, mining, and hauling ore into leaching pads. With this operation they hired and fired specialists. It always seemed that success was just around the corner.

Most of the efforts were on a trial-and-error basis, but it seems that Dame Fortune did not want to smile on such an occasion.

The knowledge and the experience of the gold leaching process had already been worked out, and the information was stored in the archives of the U.S. Bureau of Mines. The bureau offered, at no expense, to send a person specifically trained in the leaching of gold ores to help solve the problems confronting the empire mining division.

Same story—the offers were rejected.

There is no one so ignorant as the person who is too smart to learn.

The Fools and the Boss's Money
by Lorin Bunker

The Hughes empire spent about $18 million buying mining claims; this money would have been better spent if it had been given to help the ailing peanut industry. A lot of the mining property was nothing more than gravel beds. Even the cost to do the assessment work was more than the claims were worth. After they found they were stuck with a lot of worthless mining property it would have been to their advantage to have given the ground back to the Indians and take a tax write-off.

It would probably have started a war, forcing the Indians to take ownership of this property.

Milking the Empire Cow
by Lorin Bunker

Not being too smart, I thought that the empire was buying mining claims that might turn mining into a profitable venture. As a result, I referred them to a gold property that had known ore bodies and a surface vein that went seventeen ounces in silver. I gave the executives a copy of a geologist's detailed report.

Nothing came of it. I didn't even get my geologist's report back, even though I had insisted on it.

Trying to find an answer to such indignation, I went to Mr. Fred Steen, an old-timer, and asked, "Fred, what's going on in the Hughes purchase of mining properties?"

He answered, "Mr. Hughes does not know what is going on. All the parties involved are controlling the buying and selling price, and they want a kickback on top of that. They wanted my mining property, but I wouldn't deal like that. I want a clear conscience when I die and go to see my wife and son."

They milked the empire cow for about $18 million. Fred is happy. He is now with his wife and son.

The Wisdom of the Wise Perished
by Lorin Bunker

The miles of tunnels and the high mounds of earth were a reminder that Tonopah had once been a booming silver camp. The natives held to the theory that there were more minerals in the earth than had been taken out. They voiced their disapproval of the inactivity of the Hughes empire.

The empire had begun to feel the bite of the swindler, and they were reluctant to admit that they had been taken. Instead they made a feeble attempt to recoup the losses, and their feeble attempt cost them another small fortune.

An entourage of specialists from the U.S. Bureau of Mines came to Tonopah to take a look at the Hughes activity thereabouts. They saw the waste of time and money and offered their help, which was free. Their offer of help was rejected, and the empire went on losing Mr. Hughes's money.

There was no way that the Bureau of Mines agents could penetrate the curtain of secrecy that was around the guiding lights of the upper hierarchy to inform them of what was going on.

And so the losses went on and on, and the wisdom of the wise perished because the Hughes's pipeline to free knowledge was plugged up.

Probably there is a double (ha ha) woe for he who gets into a friend's pocket without permission.

Steal from a Friend
by Lorin Bunker

Mr. Cleveland was one among the many that sold the empire mining claims. His profit could be counted into millions of dollars. He really didn't need the money, and yet perhaps it was for old time's sake, as he claimed that he and Mr. Hughes were old-time buddies. They can talk it over, as they are both in that place of waiting beyond the grave.

The Scriptures say:

> Woe unto you rich men, that will not give your substance to the poor, for your riches will canker your souls; and this shall be your lamentations in the day of visitation, and of judgment, and indignation. The harvest is past, the summer is ended, and my soul is not saved.[1]
>
> Woe unto you poor men, whose hearts are not broken, whose spirits are not contrite, and whose bellies are not satisfied, and whose hands are not stayed from laying hold upon other men's goods, whose eyes are full of greediness, and who will not labor with your own hands.

Probably there is a double woe for the rich man that steals from a rich man and a triple woe for he who gets in a friend's pocket without permission.

Clint's Interview with Jim Haworth

Clint: "In other books about Howard Hughes, there is little mention of the gold for Howard Hughes that was removed from the mines. Do you know anything about it?"

Jim: "Yes, I do know about some of it at best. They [an executive office manager in Las Vegas] used to call me. He went to Tonopah, or sometimes somebody from Tonopah would bring the gold bars to his office. The Las Vegas office called me and ordered me to meet the executive and escort him to the bank with the gold bars."

"Who was that office manager?"

"Francis Fillerup, property manager for Howard Hughes."

"Was there much gold?"

"There were several trips to Las Vegas to escort Fillerup to the bank. All in all there were about twenty or thirty bars of gold worth about twenty thousand dollars each.

"What did you know of Fillerup?"

"He was property manager of all the mines and the empire Warm Springs Ranches and ranges. I met with him all the time. We became good friends. We often went on vacations together. Howard Hughes had two big homes at Lake Tahoe. They were for his executives. When we wanted to go up there, they would be all set up with a Deepfreeze full of steaks and a refrigerator full of food and the whiskey cabinet full of all kinds of liquors. Francis Fillerup was a good guy and loyal to Howard Hughes.

"In Fillerup's position, he was able to see what Gay and his Mormon Aides were doing to Hughes. Gay fired Fillerup."

In all of Hughes's secrecy, he never mentioned his belief that gold would be found in his secret empire, the mountains and ranges of the Warm Springs and Conway ranches, Jim Haworth agreed: "I know there is unfound gold in these mountains right here."

"Buy It Twice" (Gold Mining Operation)
by Lorin Bunker

It was rumored that the Tonopah King Mine was a good one. The early-day owners had supposedly struck a rich vein of ore, but because they had other good properties they let this mine lie idle.

The Tonopah King was a patented mine, but another mining company had covered the same with unpatented claims, and they were anxious to sell all of their claims to Mr. Hughes.

The buying fever was at a high pitch, and the guiding lights of the empire were considered buying for themselves the offered claims and the Tonopah King. They had bought so much so fast they had forgotten that they had already purchased this mine.

I brought it to their attention and, in doing so, felt like the biblical poor man. As the Scriptures say:

> There was a little city, and few men within it; and there came a great king against it, and besieged it, and built great bulwarks against it:
> Now there was found in it a poor, wise man, and by his wisdom he delivered the city; yet no man remembered that same poor man.

Later on, after careful consideration, I wondered if the empire wanted to be saved.

Iris's Story

Jim and Iris Haworth were raised with their tough horses on the treacherous, vast Warm Springs ranges. During Jim Haworth's life, he was known for raising fine horses. He always rode beautiful well-trained horses. Now, since a cowboy depends on his horses like his right arm, something should be said about Jim's saddle horses. Jim truly believes the beauty of a horse is what he can do. Iris, one time gave Clint Baxter the story of Jim's experiences with his favorite horse, Quedo.

Jim raised a beautiful Palomino horse, one-half Thoroughbred and one-half quarter horse. The first four years of this colt's life Jim rented him and others to amateur rodeos. This palomino gelding was never ridden to the finish during the four years he was growing up.

Then Jim finally got around to breaking him. Jim took it easy with the colt; he was five years old by then, but Jim won his confidence and added him to his string. Jim rode this horse for ten long years, catching and branding wild cattle, shipping cattle, and everything that goes with the life of a cowhorse.

This horse was finally named Quedo, which means "watch out" in Spanish. Quedo was a one-man horse. No one ever rode him except Jim. One day one of Jim's Mexican cowboys needed a horse, as his was all give-out or lame, so Jim says to this Mexican, whose name was Joe, "Get on Quedo and we'll go to Quail Spring and see what we can gather."

The cowboys had to get these two wild heifers back down the steep trail, cross the big wash, and go up the steep trail, which was a good three-quarters of a mile to the top of the rim.

Jim took the lead, driving his wild heifer on the end of his lariat. Joe got his heifer following up the steep trail.

Jim used to ride this horse for ten days at a time. He was about as tough as a horse could get and was as easy-riding as a rocking chair, one of the finest rope horses in the country.

Jim rode this great horse for several more years, till he went blind in his left eye and his legs started to stiffen up from the many years of hard use gathering wild cattle.

Jim had another special horse, a registered paint gelding named Nevada Night but nicknamed Skelter. Skelter was a big coal black with four white socks to his knees and one white spot on his left hip, with a snip on his nose. He was a beautiful horse, weighing twelve hundred pounds.

This horse was a natural cutting horse. Jim used him for years in his cattle operation. I claimed him and rode him on the range for years. He was used for everything. He was a team roping horse, head or heel, and was one of the best. He had lots of sense and tremendous speed. They used to take him down to the racetrack to try out their colts, and very few could beat him for 300 yards.

Jim says he could fill a book about the good horses he has raised and broken.

Jim and I are still raising top-quality paint horses. We keep thirty-five mares, paint, quarter, and Thoroughbred, just for brood mares, and two great paint stallions, Gambler Eagle and Moapa War Drums.

Jim Haworth with a paint horse.

Howard Hughes and Jim Haworth—1970

April 3, 1970, after a long squabble with Air West Airline management, Hughes finally acquired Air West for $89,398,096. The check was delivered to Air West with an agreement stating that Hughes would have $48 million returned to him at closing to allow for the decline in stock value since start of negotiations. Shareholders expecting $22 a share, their original value, were now delivered $8.75 a share.

Under Hughes, Jim Haworth's management of the ranch was hectic from the start. William Gay and Howard Hughes's lawyer Chester C. Davis took over the executive control of Hughes's Summa Corporation right after Hughes bought the million-acre Warm Springs Ranch and ranges. Jim was busy buying water rights and range rights for Hughes. Robert Maheu replaced Bill Gay and was Howard Hughes's top man during the years of hotel buying in Las Vegas. Then Maheu was fired and Gay and Davis took over again.

Before Howard Hughes went to Las Vegas, Jim was managing Warm Springs Ranch for Francis Taylor. Bill Gay started working for Hughes in Los Angeles as a courier for Hughes's secretary, Nadine Henley. Gay didn't know a damn thing about ranching.

In 1970, after Hughes was provided title to the Warm Springs empire and during the internal squabble between Maheu and Gay, Francis Fillerup was hired to oversee the ranches and mine operations.

Francis Fillerup was an in-between of Jim Haworth and the internal circle. Fillerup was also engaged in overseeing, without specific authority of the hotel properties.

Early in 1970 Fillerup brought to Jim a long list of specific duties. Jim took the order with a smile. He said, "I don't know who made this list, but he must have copied it from an assignment of an agriculture student who copied it out of a textbook. Not one of the Mormon aides knows which end of a cow milk comes from. If I didn't do all these things, who would?"

Fillerup, by now a friend of Jim, and said, "I know. I was embarrassed to have to bring it to you."

Haworth's Orders from Bill Gay

1. SCHEDULE AND RANCH INVENTORY—DECEMBER 31, 1973

Foreman

Assumes responsibilities of Ranch Manager (when he is absent); directs the activities of the various ranch hands; supervises farming operations; repairs and maintains equipment.

Mechanic

Maintains and repairs equipment; performs needed welding on ranch; makes parts and equipment for ranch operations.

Cowboy/Handyman

Helps maintain equipment; feeds cattle; repairs fences; performs any maintenance work required.

Irrigator

Performs irrigation work; keeps ditches in working order; controls water flow and distribution.

Handyman and Apprentice Cowboy

Helps maintain equipment; feeds cattle; repairs fences; performs any maintenance work required.

Farmer

Runs farming equipment (back hoe, caterpillar, etc.); reports to and works with foreman in the farming operations.

2. Organization Chart—Functional Description Pages

General Manager

- Reports to and is responsible and accountable to Director of Property Management Group.
- Sets Division goals and objectives.
- Establishes policies and procedures for the Division.
- Plans overall ranch activities, including budgets, purchases and sales, land use.
- Organizes the operations of the ranch.
- Staffs the ranches with necessary employees.
- Directs and coordinates the activities of the ranch manager.
- Controls and coordinates the use of all resources.

Ranch Manager

- Plans detailed ranch activities.
- Staffs the ranch with necessary help.
- Directs personnel at ranch.
- Controls the expenditures of funds, and the use of equipment.
- Handles all daily operations at the ranch as follows:

- Buys and sells cattle.
- Supervises range activities.
- Supervises water developments.
- Supervises BLM grazing rights.
- Purchases equipment.
- Oversees veterinary work.
- Purchases ranch supplies and approves all bills.
- Investigates and negotiates for possible ranch purchases.
- Oversees Taylor residence (The Hughes Mansion).
- Prepares reports on ranch progress for Director of Property Management Group.
- Turns in payroll report to accounting.
- Assists in preparation of the Division budget.
- Submits various reports required by accounting division.[2]

3. Description of Each Function and Facility

The Summa Corporation Ranching Division consists of the Warm Springs Ranch at Moapa, Nevada, and the Conaway Ranch at Caliente, Nevada, plus 728,635 acres of BLM range land in Clark and Lincoln counties. The Warm Springs Ranch has been principally used for the raising of purebred Charolais and Red Brahman cattle and the raising of fodder. The long growing season permits six to seven cuttings of alfalfa hay. The Caliente ranch has a shorter growing season and is used principally for pasture, since it is contiguous to the rangeland. However, two cuttings of hay are normally harvested before it is used as pasture. This location is especially useful for breeding and conditioning replacement heifers, since they can be kept in closer proximity to the bulls and then turned into the hills for a gradual introduction to the desert range.

The Summa ranching complex is totally oriented toward the production of cattle. All activities focus upon the preparation of cattle for market or for the sale of animals to others for breeding purposes. Since it is a specialized operation in itself, no efforts are now being made to "finish" cattle for market. Animals other than breeding stock are brought to the desirable age and weight and sold to buyers for intensive feed lot finishing. Of course, it is necessary to sell culls and aged breeding stock from time to time.

The ranch holdings include two deeded ranches located about 100 miles apart. The Warm Springs Ranch, located nine miles northwest of Glendale, consists of 1,253 deeded acres and serves as the headquarters for the entire ranching operation. The Conaway Ranch has 1,470 deeded acres and provides a base for the feeding and control of cattle in the northern sector of Summa's holdings.

Ranch Report

As of December 31, 1973, the approximate utilization of deeded land was as follows:

Warm Springs Ranch

150 acres of alfalfa
70 acres of oats which is cut for hay
400 acres permanent pasture—consists of fawn fescue, Bermuda grass, bird's-foot trefoil, and many kinds of clover
250 acres native pasture
60 acres corrals and buildings
323 acres of hills and rough pasture

Conaway Ranch
35 acres of alfalfa
400 acres of native grass meadow
110 acres of new land planted in permanent pasture, consisting of fescue, trefoil, tall wheat, oats, etc.
130 acres city property

300 acres rights-of-way
150 acres of land to be reclaimed into pasture
345 acres hills and wasteland

One of the Division's major assets is the 728,635 acres of government owned, Bureau of Land Management controlled grazing land to which Summa owns grazing and water rights.

The Bureau of Land Management (BLM) divides grazing land under its jurisdiction into allotments. As of the end of 1973, Summa's grazing privileges included:

SUMMA ALLOTMENTS	ACREAGES	ACTIVE AUM's[1]
Cliff Springs	36,608	2,043
Oak Springs	157,977	8,344
Jumbo	83,000	
Kane Springs (Jump Up)	133,000	6,000
Gold Butte	272,953	6,000[2]
Mormon Mesa	43,797	1,600[3]
	728,635	

1. An AUM (Animal Unit Monthly) is defined as the feed necessary to support a lactating cow (cow with calf) for one month. (This amount of feed usually amounts to 500 pounds of forage.)
2. Gold Butte was a desert-type range on which cattle allotments varied seasonally, depending upon rainfall. The Gold Butte allotment would vary from 120 head to 1,500 head annually. Conditional grazing allowed on Gold Butte could be conservatively calculated at 500 head year-round, or 6,000 AUMs.
3. Mormon Mesa was also considered a desert-type range on which cattle allotments vary seasonally, depending upon rainfall. The Mormon Mesa allotment would vary from 20 head to 500 head annually. Conditional grazing allowed on Mormon Mesa could be conservatively calculated at 200 head for eight months, or 1,600 AUMs. Because of its arid conditions, they normally grazed on Mormon Mesa from October to June only.

Rainfall was such in 1973 that all allotments, including Gold Butte and Mormon Mesa, were capable of sustaining their full quota of cattle with much forage to spare.

A glance at the accompanying map (Exhibit A) will show the location of the two deeded properties in relation to the BLM grazing allotments.

The basic cattle program of the Division is fourfold:

1. To raise purebred Brahman cattle, selling most of the bulls and keeping the better cows for breeding stock. This herd is now pastured at Warm Springs Ranch.
2. To raise purebred Charolais cattle, selling most of the bulls and keeping the better cows for breeding stock. The herd is also now at Warm Springs Ranch.
3. To raise a Charbray cross (Brahman bulls and Charolais cows), which are excellent beef cattle and do well in our desert and mountain ranges. However, because of the high price this cross-bred animal commands, it is sold essentially as breeding stock.
4. To raise a good grade of commercial cattle for market. These cattle are placed on the BLM grazing ranges insofar as possible. They are brought in for pasturage on hay feeding, so as to gain weight prior to sale. Normally, they are sold to feed lot buyers when they weigh about 700 pounds, or they may be sold as weaner calves.

At the present time, we have mostly Charbray and Brangus (5/8 Angus—3/8 Brahma) as grade or commercial market cattle. Through an active acquisition and culling program, we are working toward a herd of commercial Brangus cattle as well as a herd of Charbray range cattle. It is felt that, by building up our Brangus herd, we can, by the end of 1974, be selling these animals as commercial breeding stock.

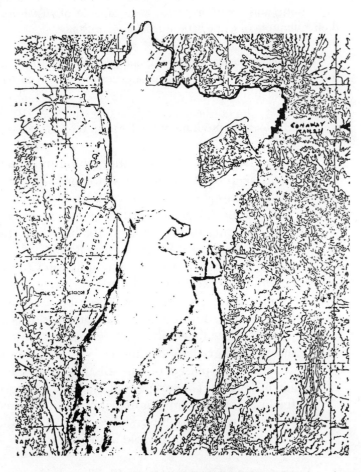

Outlined areas accentuate the Hughes Warm Springs Ranch and ranges in Las Vegas and Lake Mead area.

Improvements during the past year at Warm Springs Ranch include:

1. Approximately 1,800 tons of alfalfa, oat and grass hay were put into stacks, an increase of 600 tons over the previous year. Hay is selling at a price in excess of $60 per ton. This increase was accomplished through improved irrigation, new seeding and fertilization.
2. 45 acres of land have been cleared, leveled and put into production.
3. Two large stock yards have been built, with cattle mangers all the way around them.
4. A new roof has been put on the Taylor home. The air conditioning and heating system has been restored and the home has been painted, inside and out.
5. Our purebred herd of Charolais has been upgraded by rigid culling of old cows and inferior animals.
6. Some of the old worn out saddle horses were sold and young ones broken to replace them. Our horses are increasing, as we had a good colt crop.

Improvements during the past year at Conaway [sic] Ranch include:

1. Two wells have been drilled, one of which will be kept for culinary purposes. The other well pumps 1,800 gallons per minute and will enable us to irrigate 150 acres of new land.
2. Three old wells have been removed.
3. Ditches were put into working order, enabling us to get water to the meadows. Consequently, approximately 80 tons of hay were baled and a lot of good pasture was raised.
4. Many old fences were taken out.
5. Tons of old junk and trash were hauled off and buried.

6. The ranch house was repaired and painted, inside and out.

Range improvements during 1973 include:
1. Five mountain springs have been redeveloped and piped into stock watering troughs.
2. A 50,000 gallon tank has been moved from the Sands Hotel to the Delamar Flats. This tank will be used for storage of water from mountain springs, then piped 20 miles in two directions to stock watering troughs every 2-1/2 miles.
3. A range management agreement was entered into with BLM to improve the ranges. BLM will put in several miles of new pipe line, furnishing equipment and pipe, with Summa furnishing some of the labor.
4. Three 10,000 gallon water troughs and several miles of pipe line have been installed to bring the water to the same areas as the feed.
5. Two reservoirs have been completed which, with sufficient rainfall, should give us a year-round supply of water.
6. The Stewart Range has been purchased. For the past two years, this range was leased. One reservoir has been dug out with our bulldozer and two miles of pipe have been installed.
7. A 500 acre holding pasture with a 4 wire fence has been completed at Gold Butte Range, saving time and hay during our range round-ups in the spring and fall. There is enough water in this pasture and usually enough grass to hold 200 to 300 head of cattle for two weeks while we are shipping, branding and weaning calves.

Several miles of drift fence have been repaired, giving us

better control of the cattle. Floods had washed out 2-1/2 miles of pipe line the year before and this was replaced.

One spring was redeveloped.

Left to right: Iris Haworth, Jim Haworth, Francis Fillerup, and a Hughes executive, 1976.

As of December 31, 1973, the cattle inventory had been increased by about 1,200 head from the same date a year ago. The year end inventory was as follows:

	Cows	Calves	Heifers	Bulls	Steers	Totals
Charolais Pure-bred	106	84	44	60	-0-	294
Red Brahman	32	15	5	6	-0-	58
Range Cattle	<u>1,187</u>	<u>612</u>	<u>335</u>	<u>47</u>	<u>3</u>	<u>2,184</u>
Totals	1,325	711	384	113	3	2,536

4. **This Item Is Being Prepared and Submitted by the Accounting Division.**

5. **This Item Is Being Prepared and Submitted by the Accounting Division.**

6. **Personnel**

	1971	1972	1973
Management	1	2	2
Supervision	1	1	2
Ranch Hands[1]	5	6	9

1. Additional hands are required for seasonal peaks in the work load—particularly during the summer months when haying, cattle movement and branding require temporary helpers.

Notes

1. Scriptural quotes from the Doctorn Encovince, Sect. 56 (Verses 16 and 17).
2. Jim Haworth was flown in monthly to Gay's Los Angeles headquarters to submit reports and receive orders.

9

A Dream Comes True—Howard Hughes Buys Warm Springs

Howard Hughes's Million-Acre Empire

Before buying the Warm Springs Ranch, Howard Hughes bought the Madam Krupp Ranch complete with the madam and her mansion for $1.25 million. He also bought cattle from Jim Haworth and from Mr. Francis Taylor, owner of the Warm Springs Ranch. Before Francis Taylor died, he willed the Warm Springs Ranch to his first wife and Jim. After Taylor died, his second wife managed to change the will to her name only. She then contacted Jim to see if he could sell the ranch. Jim was contacted by Howard Hughes through executives Jack Hooper and Dick Gray, who consummated the purchase. Jim went to the Madam Krupp Ranch to manage the cattle for Mr. Hughes.

Jim's first order from Howard Hughes was in 1967 to drive several hundred head of cattle from the Warm Springs Ranch to the Madam Krupp ranch. The Krupp Ranch is on Mount Charleston. There were forty acres of good pasture besides the mansion and ranch headquarters.

With all that money and airplanes and cattle haulers, the cows and Jim could have ridden in style the ninety-five miles to the Krupp pasture. This was the beginning of Howard

Hughes's other empire, a ranch and ranges of 1 million acres, an area covering several Nevada counties and much of the entire state.

Through mismanagement by the property division, Hughes could not help but lose the majority of the Krupp cattle the first year. They did not die. These good breeding animals were taken to slaughter by Gay's men, probably for Hughes's hotel beef.

Meanwhile, several hundred thousand dollars were wasted on the Krupp ranch, fixing it up as a playhouse for Hughes's high executives from Las Vegas and Los Angeles. This was after William Gay placed himself in charge of the Summa Corporation. Robert Maheu was in on the buying of the ranch and used the mansion as his.

Summa Corporation, a subsidiary of Hughes Tool Company, was formed and run by William Gay.

Late in the summer of 1968, Mr. Hughes bought the beautiful Warm Springs Ranch of Moapa, Nevada, along with the hundreds of prize cattle that Mr. Francis Taylor and Jim, as his manager, had bred for many years. The Warm Springs Ranch was the finest ranch in the state of Nevada.

The huge purchases from Francis Taylor also included thousands of acres of choice range land, the Mormon Mesa, Gold Butte, and a northern range called Cliff Springs. Later Hughes also bought the Conway Ranch, the Oak Spring, and the Stewart ranges, all in Lincoln County. He hired Jim to run the ranch.

In February 1970, "Cow Boss" (as they called Jim) with his men made the big cattle drive for Hughes. Five hundred breeding cows were driven from Warm Springs Ranch to Gold Butte, a distance of about eighty miles, a tough four-day trip. During Jim's management of Hughes's ranches and their purchases, Howard Hughes scouted his work by air. This he did during his periods of San Limbo. Jim never talked to him.

Orders were by courier, usually Dick Gray, who flew in to visit. Also, Jim was flown to Los Angeles each month to meet with Bill Gay and his men.

Gathering wild cattle went on for the next year and a half.

Jack Hooper and Webb and Bob Morgan went up to the Conway Ranch cowboy camps for outings. They came in by Hughes helicopter and landed wherever Jim and his men were. Bob Morgan was long-time secretary-treasurer for the Hughes Tool Company in Houston.

Mike Prince, an old-timer cowboy and friend of Jim, wrote a book of poems about the area.

In Old Mesquite
From the book **Far Horizons: A Cowboy's Poetry** *by Mike Prince*

We hauled a load o'bulls
Over to Mesquite
For their annual Fair,
Rodeo and race meet

Now, these was only range bulls
They never had been bucked
Hell, for most o'them old bulls
T'was the first time they'd been trucked!

To say that they was snorty
Is puttin' it pretty mild
T'is closer to the truth
To say they was plumb wild!

We'd gathered them ol' bulls
From a range they call Gold Butte
Damn few had seen a corral
Let alone a buckin' chute!

Our rodeo was just an "Ammy"
As the pro boys scornfully say
But boys, it got plumb western
In old Mesquite that day

Most of them ol' range bulls
Sure did turn the crank
And two or three of them
You'd have to rate as rank

They was all the boys could handle
Jimmy Haworth swelled with pride
As them old bulls of his
Sure made them cowboys ride

The rodeo was nearly over
When Jimmy gave a shout
Some fool had left a gate wide open
And one of our bulls was out

Jim shook his lassa down
And me, I done the same
"We gotta catch him 'fore the river!"
I heard ol' Jim exclaim

Now, there was a field of oats
'Tween the river and that bull
That grain was three feet high
And the seed heads they was full

Down through that field we flew
Like a run-away freight train
And like a Kansas thresher
We was harvestin' that grain

I had it in my eyes and ears
And even up my nose
I had it in my boots
And deep down in my clothes

We finally roped that bull
And he put up quite a battle
But with two ropes on him
We made his old hocks rattle

At the top of that grain field
A farmer was waitin' for us
I'm here to tell ya boys . . .
That Mormon boy could cuss!

He shook his fist o'erhead
Swore he'd have us both in jail
Said they'd throw the book at us
We wouldn't be out on bail

He finally settled down
When Jimmy said he'd pay
For the damage we had done
In his grain field that day

Sure it was just an "Ammy"
As the "Professionals" say
But it was mighty western
In old Mesquite that day!

The Big Drive

During the first day to Gold Butte Jim and the boys made it to the big reservoir on Mormon Mesa. They made camp at dark and were able to corral all the cattle there overnight. Next morning before daylight, horses were saddled up while one of the cowboys was cooking breakfast.

When the empire went into the ranching business, they had big plans in mind, such as building new corrals, repairing drift fences, springs, and water holes, but dreams and plans often go astray, especially when the top brass suddenly lose interest and tighten the strings on the money purse even tighter. Consequently the cattle and the range suffered. Thirsty cows and horses fought over the small trickles of water from springs that ran for a few rods and sank into the sand, only to go back into the desert with thirst unquenched. What little money was needed to develop a fine setup for the cattle was likely used for an unneeded carpet in one of the empire's casinos or to line one of the executive's pockets. What the hell . . . the springs had been the same for the past hundred years, so what needed changing now?

Being part of a multi-million-dollar outfit, Jim thought he could relieve the strains on the ranch, but soon found that those in command had no intention of helping Mr. Hughes make the ranch a pleasure and success. With unlimited money to buy cattle trucks to haul the livestock, Jim was disappointed and had to drive 500 head of cattle from the Warm Springs Ranch to the range at Gold Butte (a distance of eighty miles) in February of 1970.

It took four days to make the trek, and to this day Jim is often reminded of that first night. The weather was bad and they made camp about dark at the big reservoir on Mormon Mesa. None of the cowboys was in much of a mood to eat, they were so tired. A snorty old snide Jim called Budweiser deprived them of their breakfast the next morning. Jim cinched him up intending to let him "soak" while they ate. He exploded with the first tight jerk of the riggin' and bucked through the camp, scattering bacon and eggs, coffee, and biscuits all over the desert, the result being five cowboys had to drive the herd across the long stretch of desert with their stomachs still flapping against their backbones.

Ranges of Howard Hughes's Warm Springs Ranch.

It was a trip Jim would never forget. When they reached the Virgin River, the water was ragin' like a mad bull. It sure took some horse persuasion to get them cattle to cross that tumblin' hell. Before they got the job done, they were a bunch of miserable, cold, wet, and tired cowpunchers.

The chuck wagon met them after dark at Juanita Springs on the lower steps of the Bunkerville Mountain. There were about a hundred and sixty acres of partially fenced land around the spring, and Jim thought that it would be a likely place to hold the herd for the night. They pitched their camp in a fenced area. After the horses were cared for, they prepared and wolfed a good dutch-oven supper, then settled down for the night.

Old Blue, Jim's good old cow dog, put himself alongside his bedroll to sleep, and all went well until about four o'clock in the mornin', when a curious old Brahma cow walked up and sniffed at Jim's blankets. Old Blue grabbed her by the nose, and all hell broke loose. She carried him down through the herd, bawling her head off and clawing the air like a climbing tiger tryin' to get loose from his locked fangs. Well, needless to say, between the two of them, they started one of the worst stampedes Jim ever witnessed. Five hundred head of cows laid the fence flat and were headed for parts unknown in no time. They saddled up and got right after them, but it was noon the next day before they finally got the cattle all rounded up and had them once more on the trail to Gold Butte, minus breakfast and all.

They were two more days on that dry, dusty desert before they finally got the cattle located on the range that was to be their home for some time to come. Jim sure hoped Mr. Hughes appreciated the things they had to go through to see his cattle were taken care of. Where he was, though, he probably didn't have any idea of the problems they had doin' it.

Mr. Hughes would say, "I sure wish I'd have known when I was down there what ranch living was like. That's where I'd have spent my time instead of the Bahamas or Acapulco. I wish I had some way of showing that ranch manager of mine how much it means to me for him to look out for my interests the way he did. Some business, that ranch life. It appears to me it'd make a real man out of a weakling."

To paraphrase the Apostle Paul, "It can be said that your cowboys covet no man's silver and gold, from what I've seen." A dry comment. They give an honest day's work for an honest day's pay, quite unlike some of the empire's other employees, it appeared to Jim. One wise man said, "If your labors don't bring your employer a profit, at least let your efforts save him from any losses," and from what Jim saw, them cowpunchers were doin' their very best.

Hell, those ranch hands never read the Scriptures or ever heard the words of that wise man.

It's a strange thing, but at one time or another, most everyone likes to think they are, or would like to be, a cowboy. Lot's of 'em have tried and were sure disappointed to find their fear plumb overcame their courage, but still, the toughest ones have ridden on barstools down there, and it 'pears to Jim the drugstore cowboys far outnumber the real ones.

The Warm Springs Ranch operation likely cost considerable more because of the would-be cowpokes sent to help Jim. There were some who were utterly useless—like this one feller. He wasn't as smart as the horse Jim gave him to ride, and the horse wasn't smart enough to know how stupid the dude was, where horse know-how was concerned. Tybo was a good nag, strong and quiet and gentle by nature. His greatest fault was putting his trust in his rider, and the next one was his slowness to respond to the reins. The old feller relied solely upon his rider to keep him out of trouble.

Jim don't know how it came about, but one day the dude accidentally roped a two-year-old Brahma heifer with mighty sharp horns, then just as accidentally got some dallies around the horn. Well, when that heifer hit the end of the rope a time or two, her blood got stirred up some, and she was on the prod in no time. Figurin' old Tybo was sure the cause of all her

Jim Haworth drawing, "Trouble in the Making."

trouble, she charged him and hit him broadside with her shoulder as she went past. That old good-natured snide just grunted and stood flat-footed where he was, expectin' the cowboy aboard would let him know what he was to do next.

Well, the dude didn't *know* what to do next, and the heifer took the advantage. She whirled and charged Tybo again but came up on the opposite side, bringing the rope around behind him right under his tail, then gouged him in the belly with them two sharp horns. Tybo knew then he was on his own,

Jim Haworth drawing, "The Bronc Buster."

and the natural thing for a horse to do when in doubt and having severe pain inflicted on him at the same time is to buck his way out of his predicament. And that's just what Tybo did. The rope under his tail didn't help matters none; as a matter of fact, he exploded a little higher into the air, and because of it, the dude lost all holds, including the reins, his dallies, and stirrups, and looked elsewhere for his salvation. There was none handy, and he ended up on the ground on his tailbone while Tybo bucked free off into the desert.

The heifer, free from saddle horn and still on the prod, stood her head up looking for someone to vent her wrath on, and seeing the dude on the ground, she charged him. He tried to scramble for safety, but she was determined to get her licks in and sniffed at the seat of his pants, time and again, to show him she meant business. He finally sprawled on his face in the dirt, and she jumped over him with one great, big snort, just barely clearing him with her heels as she kicked high into the air and headed into the desert dragging a rope.

Well, the dude sure didn't have any appreciation for the chance Jim tried to give him to become a real cowboy. He cussed Jim and his right-hand man something awful for givin' him a raw bronc to ride. He was plumb insulted when they laughed good-naturedly at him, too, when they realized he'd come out of the incident with nothin' hurt but his pride. "Just funnin'," they told him. They'd be glad to capture old Tybo so he could catch that young heifer again and get his revenge. He stormed off to sulk in the shade of a Joshua tree close by. Nothin' real bad come of it, but it sure cured him from wantin' to become a cowpuncher.

When Clint heard the tale, he chuckled in amusement. "That scene would bring more laughs than any movie Howard ever made. Say, can you give me any more such stories? And I'd like to use some of your great drawings."

"Hell, yes," says Jim. "I've got lots of 'em here in my book. Wanta hear more?"

Haworth Injured in Cattle Drive

(Newspaper Article, about 1981—out of business *Moapa Valley Progress)*
Jim Haworth and Newt Bundy moving cattle at the Warm Springs Ranch were flipping their ropes to help head the cows when through a freak accident Jim's horse was flipped to the ground. It was believed Jim's horse stepped in the loop thrown by Newt and then both horses started bucking and as the rope tightened the one horse was thrown to the ground. Jim was

knocked out, as the horse half rolled on him and kicked him in the head.

Jim underwent surgery on Monday morning and it was reported he was very lucky as the shoulder socket could be repaired, and a pin was put in the break in the arm. There was no concussion from the head injury, but a bump and two black eyes plus lots of soreness didn't help his overall misery. He expects to be home for Christmas.

Jim and wife Iris Haworth are residents of Warm Springs, they have two grown children, Rita Tobiasson of Warm Springs and Jerry Haworth of Logandale, and grandchildren.

Ropin' and Wranglin' on Hughes's Warm Springs Ranges

Jim and Iris Haworth were born and raised on the vast Warm Springs Ranch and ranges. They lived as ranchers with their cowboys and their tough horses in the treacherous Nevada mountains and ranges.

Jim always believed the beauty of a horse is his performance. Iris, one time told Clint her story of Jim's experiences with his favorite horse, "Quedo."

This horse was finally named "Quedo," which means "watch out" in Spanish. Quedo was a one-man horse. No one ever rode him except Jim. One day one of Jim's Mexican cowboys needed a horse, as his string was all "gave-out" or lame so Jim says to this Mexican, whose name was Joe, "Get on Quedo and we'll go to Quail Spring and see what we can gather."

Quail Spring ran out of the bottom of a deep box canyon filled with mesquite and catclaw trees and certain times of the year when the mesquite beans were ripe, the wild cattle would

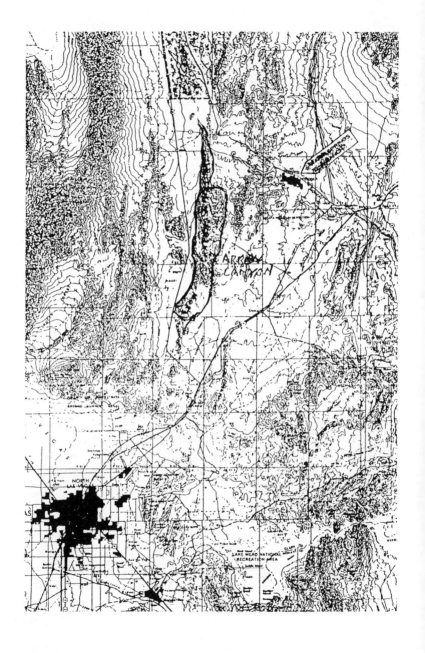

congregate in this hell hole of the desert range known as Gold Butte.

Joe and Jim saddled up and headed for Quail Canyon. Quedo was a perfect gentleman on the five-mile ride to Quail Canyon.

Jim relates, "As we rode along the rim of the canyon, we could see a small bunch of wild cattle about a half mile below the canyon rim. They saw us and began to mill around in the mesquite thickets in the bottom of Quail Canyon. Joe and I slipped round below the little bunch of cattle and felt our way down the steep trail to the canyon floor. Here came the wild bunch, headed for Lake Mead, which was about ten miles away.

"I roped a three year old steer. Joe put his riata on a three or four year old long-eared heifer. We jerked these wild animals down and tied their hind legs together, so they couldn't travel.

"Then Joe and I picked up the trail at a high gallop. Within a mile the cowboys spotted the cattle climbing out of the canyon up a steep trail almost too steep for the horses to climb out. So the Mexican cowboy and I followed the herd on out on top of canyon rim where I roped another long-eared heifer and Joe caught a slick yearling heifer."

Old Budweiser, a bay horse of Jim's, was a little snorty when his cinch was pulled up. He exploded, bucking all through the camp, scattering coffee, bacon and eggs all over the desert.

The result was five cowboys had to leave without breakfast and head across the long dry stretch of the Mormon Mesa and down a long canyon to the Virgin River, where high water was racing. The 500 cows were finally made to cross the river without any loss, just some cold and wet cowboys.

Then the work began and the fun was over, the wild cattle

Jim Haworth drawing, "Old Budweiser for Breakfast."

Jim Haworth drawing, "Fording the Virgin River."

Jim Haworth drawing, "Cow Camp."

had to be led back to a corral where they would be branded and loaded on a truck to be hauled out later.

There was a good corral about a mile or so from the canyon rim, called Mockingbird Spring.

The cowboys had to get these two wild heifers back up the steep trail and a good three-quarters of a mile to the top of the rim.

Jim Haworth drawing, "The Mexican Cowboy."

Jim took the lead driving his wild heifer on the end of his lariat. Joe got his heifer following up the steep trail.

Jim heard a commotion behind him. When he looked around he saw the Mexican cowboy, Joe, flying high in the air.

Quedo had enough of him and let him down in a pile of boulders on his head. The Mexican lay there for a little while. Jim thought he had been killed, but pretty soon Joe started to kicking like a chicken. Jim got off his horse and helped his partner up, but couldn't get Joe back on Quedo so he had to trade horses with Joe and continue on their slow climb up the canyon wall. Jim said none of the other cowboys wanted to ride Quedo after that.

Jim used to ride Quedo for ten days at a time, he was about as tough as a horse could get and was as easy riding as a rocking chair. He was one of the finest roping horses in the country.

Jim rode this great horse for several more years till he went blind in his left eye and his legs had started to stiffen up from the many years of hard use gathering wild cattle.

Jim sold Quedo along with some more horses to a big rodeo producer, and Quedo ended up in a bucking string, he turned out to be one of the nation's top saddle bronc horses. He was chosen for the National Finals Rodeo five different years. The last time Jim saw him, which was at the N.F.R. in Las Vegas, Nevada, the old horse was 25 years old. At that time he was fat and slick. Those rodeo people took the best care of him. He bucked about 15 minutes a month. This great horse had his name changed to "Big Casino" after becoming a famous bucking horse.

Jim had another special horse, a registered paint gelding he named "Nevada Night," but Iris nicknamed him "Skelter." Skelter was a big coal black with four white socks to his knees, one white spot on his left hip with a white swipe on his nose. He was a beautiful horse, weighing over 1200 pounds.

This horse was a natural cutting horse. Jim used him for years in his cattle operation. His wife claimed him and rode him on the range for years. He was used for everything, he was a team roping horse, head or heel, and was one of the best. He had lots of sense and tremendous speed. They used to take him down to the racetrack to try their colts out and very few could beat him for 300 yards.

Jim says he could fill a book about the good horses he has raised and broken.

Jim and Iris, are still raising top quality paint horses. They keep thirty-five mares, paint, quarter and Thoroughbred, just for brood mares and two great paint stallions, "Gambler Eagle" and "Moapa War Drums."

I am sure that if Mr. Hughes could have been turned loose by his Mormon aides and lived on Warm Springs Ranch before being drugged and destroyed, he would be alive today and a very happy man.

10

The Warm Springs Ranch and Hughes's Executives' Involvement During Hughes's Self-Imposed Asylum

After the 1970 final purchase of the Warm Springs Ranch (under the name of Hughes Tool Company, Howard Hughes negotiated for the ranch August 20, 1968, but the final sale and deed were recorded July 29, 1970), the higher-ups in the Hughes organization became more interested in the Hughes Warm Springs empire. Robert Maheu had been ousted, and Bill Gay took over as top executive for Hughes. Jim Haworth was sent a message to meet with them at the great white mausoleum, the Hughes operations headquarters at 7000 Romaine Street, Los Angeles. Thereafter, Jim met with them almost monthly to discuss the Warm Springs Ranch operation and acquisitions. During this time Bill Gay and his assistants were in charge.

Hughes's attorney, Dick Gray was executive manager of the ranch and would fly by Hughes's helicopter to visit the ranch. He directed his pilot to land where Jim was working cattle out on the range. Jim even herded the cattle with the Hughes helicopter. That saved a lot of tough riding.

Dick Gray and Jim became good friends. They had barbecues together with other executives joining in. Dick Gray died May 7, 1975, of a heart attack, forty-nine years old, and Bill Gay's assistants took over. Jim did not realize the strong arm Bill Gay used in dealing with Howard Hughes and his money.

Howard Hughes heard of the book Jim was writing about his other empire. Jim passed a copy to him by courier. He never heard from Hughes but is sure he never saw the book. Hughes's secret Warm Springs empire was distanced from Howard Hughes until he died. Also, his directives for Jim never reached him. The once-brilliant mind of Howard Hughes was so deadened by ample supplies of cocaine that he became distrustful of everyone and sought seclusion in his penthouse suite of the Desert Inn Hotel. He didn't even want to see Jean Peters. Stories Jim heard about Howard Hughes's strange behavior in his last years may be true, but they are not indicative of the real Howard Hughes for whom he worked.

After Gay took over ranch business from Howard Hughes, the first thing he did was sell off the valuable Brahma cattle that Frank Taylor and Jim had developed. They didn't know a damn thing about ranching.

In the seventies Howard Hughes, busy with all his irons in the fire, became depressed. He dreamed of his San Limbo getaways flying over the ranch. Jim was busy finding springs to water the cattle and putting in miles of water pipe.

Francis Fillerup was placed in charge of all the ranch properties. He was also property manager of all Hughes's Las Vegas properties, including other landholdings, gold mines, etc. Fillerup often visited the ranch, and he and Jim occasionally socialized together at Hughes's mansion at Lake Tahoe. They also went on cattle buying trips together.

Howard Hughes's ranch purchasing agent, Francis Fillerup, often took Jim on flying missions to buy cattle and ranches for Hughes, supposedly on Hughes's orders.

Jim told Clint about a Montana cattle buying trip.

"Who was it went with you on this?"

"Fillerup, Hughes's property manager, got the jet, Hughes's Lear jet, and pilot and we flew up to this ranch in Montana to look at these cattle he was going to buy for us.

"We lit on this damn Indian reservation, and when the pilot decided we couldn't take off from that airport because there was a huge pile of boulders off the little strip there and with our weight we couldn't get back in the air the pilot had to fly to Cutbank, Montana, where there was a good airstrip. So, we stayed up in that Indian camp overnight in a little old cabin."

"Just the two of you?"

"Four of us."

Clint asked Iris, "You went, too?"

Iris piped up, "Yeah, I was with Jim. Yes, Mr. Fillerup and his wife, Sandy, and Jim and I. We landed on the reservation in Montana, next to Glacier Park."

"Well," Jim continued, "the rancher never did show up to meet us, so we gave those Indians five dollars to haul us into town. We got in the back of that old car full of beer cans and bottles and we bounced all over the place until we got into town, the town of Saint Mary's, Montana. The pilot took off with the plane to land on a better strip near town and pick us up there; then the Indian hauled us over to Cutbank, where the plane could take off with us. That was Hughes's Lear jet. We left without seeing the cattle or the ranch foreman.

"Then I went to Denver buying cattle with Fillerup, the supervisor, one time, buying bulls, in that Lear jet. Then I went to Kurrville, Texas, to a big ranch facility, me and Allen Stroud, another of Gay's men. We went down there buying cattle, took that jet down there. We used to also round up Hughes's cattle with the helicopter. That was the easy way."

Summa Corporation Brands for the Warm Springs Ranch

Recorded Hughes Ranch Brands

Horse Brand Left Hip	— S —	Bar S Bar
Cattle Brand Left Hip	C	Quarter Circle C
Cattle Brand (purebred Brahmas)	AAA	Triple A
Cattle Brand	✠◇✠	Cross Diamond Cross
Jim Haworth's Horse and Cattle Brand	5/7	Five Slash Seven

Haworth on Hughes's Range

At this point, Jim was pretty sure Howard Hughes was in control of the ranches in spite of Gay's interference and Maheu's exodus.

In 1972, Mr. C. D. Stewart got in touch with Jim. He had a fine piece of range land in the Kane Springs Valley and on into the Delamar Mountains. Jim told "Hughes's people" at their monthly meeting about the deal, and in a very short time he had bought the Stewart range.

Jim spent many months getting range rights and traveling to Carson City, capital of Nevada, writing letters, and appearing at the Las Vegas Hughes office. He never met or talked to Howard Hughes. The business of the monthly meetings was relayed to Hughes by his guards.

By this time the Hughes ranching empire extended for around two hundred miles, almost a million acres, two of the best ranches in the state of Nevada, with 4,000 head of fine cattle.

The Hughes people bought more ranch property to supply beef and food for his big Hughes hotels in Las Vegas, which would have saved the Hughes hotel empire millions of dollars and also put the ranching division in a real paying situation. This would have dwarfed the beef production for hotels that Binion was facilitating for his luxurious Horseshoe Hotel.

They drilled many good water wells for the ranch and planted hundreds of acres of ranch land into alfalfa and permanent pastures. They also did a tremendous amount of rangeland improvements. They put in miles and miles of water pipelines, big water storage tanks, reservoirs, and fences and made for Mr. Hughes the finest ranges in the state.

Jim knows now, as Mr. Hughes looks down on his fine ranches and his vast rangelands filled with beautiful cattle and horses, that he is well pleased that he had some hard-working, honest men looking after the inside of his other empire.

The Conway Ranch

In 1973, Jim heard about the Conway Ranch being for sale, so again he went to the powers that be and again they let him buy the ranch and a beautiful range that tied up with the rest of their rangeland.

Jim was ordered by Howard Hughes to get water and range rights from the BLM for the thousands of acres of graze land.

The Conway Ranch, located in Lincoln County near Caliente, Nevada, was purchased by Jim for Howard Hughes in 1973. The Conway cattle were branded with (Circle C) by Jim and his cowboys.

The headquarters was located in the beautiful Meadow

Valley Wash. The Conway cattle range extended into the Delamar Mountains and adjacent flats.

After Emery Conway sold the ranch to the Howard Hughes empire, he went to work for the Hughes Company. Emery's experience and knowledge was a valuable asset to Howard Hughes. Emery did not complain even if his wages were not equal to those of a Landmark Hotel cook.

The years and the weather left their marks on Emery, but instead of turning him sour, the experiences mellowed him. He served without pay on farm boards and committees to the benefit of the other ranchers and the public. Service was more important to him than wealth or fame. Emery's word was good as his bond. He was the most mild-mannered, kind, helpful person one would ever hope to meet.

The mystery is how a person so much a gentleman could raise such wild and mean cattle. Even after several years, Mr. Hughes's cowboys were trying to catch some of those wild cattle—and they slowly succeeded.

Emery helped the cowboys when he was needed and extended his sympathy to them.

It was up to Jim to make the deal with Emery Conway for his ranch. Hughes paid Conway $1 million for the entire Conway Ranch. (The ranch was also called Conaway Ranch.) Emery was ready to retire, but he still remained on the ranch doing what he could. A couple hundred head of cattle were "throwed" in the deal. They were wild ones running on the mountains that nobody had even branded.

So, the first two or three months they were rounding up these cattle and hauling them to market. That's when Lorin Bunker came to work for Jim 'cause the Las Vegas Hughes operations had no place for him after the gold mines failed. Lorin Bunker became a dear friend, and he and Jim still get together.

Lorin was driving the truck out there while Jim and two

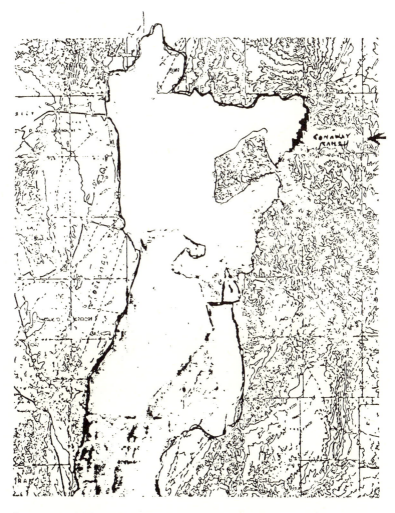
Conway and Warm Springs ranches and ranges on Howard Hughes's million-acre empire.

or three cowboys were catching those wild cattle and heading them off the mountain down to where they could load them in those in big semi trucks to haul them in for slaughter. They didn't brand these cattle. Most of them weren't any good anyhow. They were scrubby Herefords and they weren't running that breed anyway.

Lorin retired two or three years before Howard Hughes died.

Jim Haworth drawing, "The Bulls Are Beginning to Argue."

Gentleman Emery
by Lorin Bunker

Jim was instrumental in helping the Hughes empire buy

the Conway Ranch. This ranch branded their cattle with a quarter-circle C.

This beautiful ranch was in Lincoln County, Nevada, and the cattle ranged on the Delamar flats and adjacent mountains. It was a rough country, and a lot of the cattle went wild.

Jim Haworth drawing, "Dust on the Trail."

A Cowboy's Need—A Cow's Wish

Lorin Bunker states, "Emery always maintained that when the Lord made the Earth He took the parts that were left over and dumped them into the lower end of the Delamar Mountains, which consists mostly or rocks and boulders of all sizes. Between the rocks the Lord planted sage and cedars and piñons and other tough plants. In places the cedars and piñons are so thick that the sun never touches the ground. In a few places trickles of water bubble from between the boulders. It is aptly called the badlands.

"No self-respecting cow stays in this area. However, cougars, coyotes, jackrabbits, deer, wild cattle, and wild horses have made this their refuge.

"If Mr. Hughes had been properly informed by his executives of the ruggedness of this area, he might have turned his inventive mind to something to protect the cowboys when riding the range hereabouts.

"Their chaps served a good purpose, but what is needed is a helmet, a chest protector, and a quick-opening parachute of some kind."

One time, while working cattle in this area of trees and rocks, Jim was riding Quedo in a high-speed chase and was practically on the tail of a wild cow and had to stay with it until the trees thinned out so he could cast a loop. About this time, Quedo stumbled and fell and Jim was thrown head over heels high into the air. The only thing that saved him from injury was a tree, for he landed in the top of a cedar.

He was some scratched up, and the chase ended. The cow was long gone.

A Happy Family on the Conway Ranch *by Lorin Bunker*

Kim Jensen is a racehorse trainer turned to nursing cows. He is small, very strong, wiry, and determined. Weather has bleached his hair and peeled his face. There isn't much that Kim can't do with a horse or a cow, with his own lariat. He has a special talent for fixing broken water lines on the range, and he is a master mechanic when it comes to patching things up with baling wire, for the budget does not allow him any other way.

The frustrations of the job have not changed his sense of humor and have not, as yet, made him impatient of his job.

Jim hired Kim to take care of the cattle and headquartered him at the Conway Ranch.

Jim Haworth drawing, "Old Jim Almost Meets His Maker."

Jim Haworth drawing, "Old Jim Makes a Landing Pad for His Horse."

Jim Haworth drawing, "Kim Lookin' for Heaven or Hell."

Kim has a lovely wife and four small children. His thrifty wife raises chickens, pigs, and sheep and has a garden to supplement the family income. Kim's wages are not as good as that of a crap dealer's even though the responsibilities are much greater and the hours much longer.

Kim's marriage is not on the rocks in spite of the fact that he spends more time with the cows than he does with his wife.

Ranching an Empire for a Billionaire

While Jim was running the Home Ranch for Howard Hughes, Iris and he relied heavily on their Bible teachings to time crop planting and harvesting. The Scriptures say that "to everything there is a season, and a time to every purpose under heaven: A time to be born, and a time to die; a time to plant and a time to pluck, a time to weep and a time to mourn; a time to love."

Jim found early that there is a time to hold weaners and a time to sell them. He always studied the market trends so he could sell the stock at the best price. There came a bad year and the price of stock was down. Experience told Jim to buy right and hold the calves until the price increased and their extra weight of two pounds a day brought extra profit. However, the powers in the upper echelon of the Hughes executives didn't understand this. They gave orders to sell, perhaps because the casinos in the Frontier and Desert Inn were not doing well. They didn't realize to give a cow a chance. She'll make you money if you don't trade her off for a deck of cards or spin of the roulette wheel. Jim did hear later that the casinos made hundreds of thousands of dollars each year for Howard Hughes.

Dick Gray was the one that used to go out on the range with Jim all the time; they would come after Jim with helicopters. Old Hughes would have a message for him, something for him to do. Dick was the executive Hughes originally sent to check into the buying of Warm Springs Ranch. He was Hughes's lawyer from Houston.

They would leave word on the map of the Warm Springs Ranch and ranges hung on the ranch office wall about where they'd be. Dick wanted to go up and stay for a week, but then he never did get to because that Hughes helicopter would show up and pick him up. Hughes's pilot would bring Dick and drop him off and then come back and get him. Jim camped wherever they were working the cattle, sometimes a hundred miles from home. It was just wherever they happened to be out with the cattle. They'd go out and stay a week or two at a time and then move to different springs up there.

That's when Iris and Jim decided on the name the Other Side of the Empire, because nobody knew that Howard had things like this, another interesting life besides his hotels.

Clint asked Jim, "Did you ever have a telephone call from Howard?"

"I dealt with that lawyer, Chester Davis, in LA for all the different things, and when Hughes was down in the Bahamas I got a message that Howard Hughes wanted to know all about the ranch and a kind of a history of it, so that's when I wrote that history of it and sent it down to the Vegas office."

Executives and the Ranch

Bill Gay, on his own, moved the Los Angeles Division of Hughes Tool Company operations to his own new offices in the San Fernando Valley and renamed the Hughes Tool Company the Summa Corporation with his own executives and aides, much to Howard Hughes's disgust and against his will. From here on Gay held monthly meetings with Jim Haworth at the 7000 Romaine Street headquarters, now called the operations center.

After Bob Maheu was fired in 1970, Jim Haworth's responsibilities to Howard Hughes became Jim's own responsibilities. Bill Gay had little to do with the ranch.

Hughes frequently sent his helicopter and personal pilot and Dick Gray, who was in charge, to find Jim, wherever he might be on the vast million acres. The message was for Gray to immediately return to Las Vegas.

Dick Gray often went alone to the ranch to visit and play cowboy. After all, he was the Hughes property manager. Sometimes (often), Gray would be out on the range with Jim where the cowboys were rounding up cattle via helicopter. Jim liked herding cattle by airplane, the easy way.

Gray fancied himself a real cowboy. One time he made a special trip to Texas to buy a fancy cowboy outfit. His first experience with the new saddle and rope on his own horse had a horrible ending with a steer jerking Dick off the horse. Dick unknowingly had fasted the lariat to the saddle horn. After he lassoed the steer, the horse got twisted in the rope and the raging steer pulled the horse, the saddle, and Gray to the ground. After rescuing Dick Gray, Jim drew a sketch of the incident. All had a good laugh, except Gray.

Howard Hughes never visited Jim or spoke to him by phone. Bill Gay and his aides controlled all of Howard Hughes's business but never had a signed contract. Earlier, Howard Hughes had contracted with Maheu and made him "his alter ego," his spokesman, resulting in the Gay-Maheu controversy over control that resulted in the firing of Maheu. One time Maheu visited the ranch (helicopter) with the Hughes pilot.

While the Cat's Away

During the sixties and seventies Jim Haworth had some tough encounters with the people under Bill Gay. After a hard day on the range Jim set to drawing charcoal sketches to settle his nerves. With his cowboys he sat hunched over a bright mesquite fire. He took his drawin' board and paper. He used charcoal to make the drawin's of pictures that flashed through his mind.

There were always interruptions by the boys and their

stories. Lonesome cowboys always like to tell of their conquests of pretty barroom maidens. Some wrote pretty fair stories of their Warm Springs Ranch experiences while working for Howard Hughes.

In addition to his management of the ranch, Jim was engaged in travel to other states buying more good Hughes cattle for breeding and show.

The original Hughes cattle were bought from Taylor and Jim by Hooper and Gray for Hughes's Madam Krupp Ranch. Jim Gardenshire was the Krupp ranch manager during that time.

Dick Gray went, on Hughes's orders, to Frank Taylor's widow to arrange purchase of her Warm Springs Ranch. The ranch was purchased by Howard Hughes's Hughes Tool Company, which he owned totally, for the sum of $2,500,000. The ranch was bought by negotiations of Dick Gray and Bob Morgan, executives, with Taylor's widow.

Jerky Gravy

While watching the campfire after the cowboys turned in, Jim Haworth dug out his favorite recipe. After reading it, he had a snack of jerky gravy on sour dough bread.

Jim's Jerky Gravy Recipe

Without refrigeration meat will spoil if it is not taken care of. It should be hung out during the cold nights and wrapped in a canvas during the warm days.

Then some of the meat should be cut in strips and sprinkled with salt and pepper and put on a wire line to dry.

This jerky makes good eating during the day when you are a long way from camp.

You have heard of the French chefs and their fine fancy food, but none of it can beat some jerky gravy. Colonel Sanders has his secret formula to fry chickens, but there is no secret to jerky gravy.

First you pound up into a powder a double handful of this dried meat, then put it in some water to soak while you make the gravy out of shortening, flour, and water. Keep stirring and add the meat and cook until it comes to a thick paste.

Eat it as it is or over bread or potatoes.

The second and third helpings are just as tasty as the first. There are never any leftovers.

Then find a soft rock for a pillow, pull your hat over your eyes, and get a good night's sleep.

This is a meal that is a gourmet delight and will stick to your ribs and keep your energy fired up.

If Mr. Hughes had had some of this gravy instead of the fancy food out of the Desert Inn, he could have gotten out of his sickbed.

Hungry Coyote, Angry Dog

This day's ride to gather cattle started out at sunrise, but it was rudely interrupted. Kim's dog jumped a long, lean, hungry coyote. Kim yelled, "Get 'em, boy."

Kim's dog was as dedicated as Kim was to killing that coyote. In fact, they both seemed heartless. The coyote was determined to live and help out, with the ecology favoring his race.

Thus the dog and coyote fought, lunging at each other, growling and snarling, tearing at each other with sharp teeth.

Kim kept encouraging the dog, but the dog didn't seem to need it. The cowboys gathered around in a circle on their horses and respectfully watched the battle. The dog was victorious.

Before the day was over, Clint had a better understanding of Kim and the boys' hatred of the lowly coyote. He saw calves with their tails chewed off, not even leaving a stub. Others had a chunk chewed from their hindquarters. There were others he did not see, for they had not survived the vicious attack.

If those coyotes had been faithful to the laws of ecology and stayed to their calling, chasing jackrabbits, they would have been welcome on the range.

Jim Haworth drawing, "Old Blue in Hot Pursuit."

Horse Power

The two boys from Caliente Town were long on nerve and short on judgment. They really didn't need the meat, but they thought that it would be fun to go poach a deer. To fortify themselves for the trip they took a quart of hundred-proof corn juice, but failed to fill the gas tank on the dune buggy.

By noon they were riding recklessly over the old abandoned roads on the Delamar Mountains. Every sip of corn whiskey seemed to smooth out the rough roads, and they drove faster. The roar of the dune buggy engine echoed and reechoed through the mountains, and the deer, cougars, and rabbits fled from the unseen dangers. Even the blue jays took flight, squawking their complaints.

Kim was at Abandoned Spring checking for cattle when he heard the noise, and it sounded like the clattering wheels of hell. Suddenly everything became silent and the mountain returned to its normal state of serenity.

Kim was not curious by nature, but he had a feeling that someone must be in trouble with such sudden silence and went to investigate. When he found the outfit it had left the road and was resting in a pile of boulders. Their bottle was empty, they had lost their guns, the gas tank was ruptured, and the battery had fallen out and split open. The boys were sobering up, and the forty-horsepower motor was reduced to zero horsepower.

Kim sat on his horse and surveyed the scene and then quietly remarked, "This looks like the end of the trail and the beginning of a long hike for you."

They began to mumble and justify their sins, but they got no sympathy from Kim. He said, "It's all right with me if you kill yourselves and scare hell out of all the game, but I don't want you scaring Mr. Hughes's cows into a state of abortion."

To make a long story short, they promised never to return

if Kim would help them out of their predicament and not report them to the game warden.

Kim agreed and took his lasso rope and tied it to the dune buggy and pulled it out of the boulders. With two sober and repentant hunters sitting in the dune buggy, Kim towed it down the mountain with his horse.

It was one horse pulling an outfit that a short hour before had been a forty-horsepower unit.

Bermuda Triangle

There is a lot of mystery surrounding the Bermuda Triangle. Ships and airplanes suddenly disappear there without any reasonable answer. Few people have lived, and those that have tell hair-raising tales about the malfunction of safety devices.

The cowboys don't know much about the Bermuda Triangle, but they understand the principle of the triangle and the safety measures involved.

To begin with, the wild bull did not have a mark or brand on him. He was a throwback to some of the pure Conway strain of cattle and had inherited a lot of size and meanness. Kim was the first one to rope him and for safety's sake rode around a cedar tree. When the other cowboys arrived in several directions, from chasing cattle, they prepared to take the bull a couple of miles to where the truck was located.

By this time that bull was on the prod; no one horse or cowboy could handle him. To safely start the journey to the truck the cowboys put two ropes around his horns, each rope going to the horn of a saddle. On one hind leg of the bull another rope was attached, it going to another cowboy on a horse. This kept the bull from running over the two cowboys out in the lead position.

It was a slow, laborious journey with all kinds of hazards—one broken rope would have put all the cowboys to flight. A bull triangle they understand; they could care less about the Bermuda Triangle.

No Appreciation

The old long-horned cow was stuck in the mud on the shore of the reservoir. After struggling for a while, she became firmly lodged in the claylike mud and it held her in a viselike grip.

The other cows had quenched their thirst and returned to the hills. Her calf stood at a distance, bawling, waiting for her to come.

Kim and Jim came along and surveyed the scene and immediately went to work. With bare hands they dug the clinging mud from the cow's legs. Then, with two lariats tied to their horses, they dragged her from the mud with their horses.

The cow, like a lot of people, didn't show her appreciation. She tried to fight them when they took the ropes from her horns to free her.

Taking Care of Mother

The cow was old and each year she had faithfully fulfilled her mission and given Mr. Hughes another calf. She was never a gentle cow but was wild and independent.

It was in the fall of the year and the calf was about six months old when Kim and Jim noticed that she was moving slowly along the trails behind her calf. Knowing that something was wrong, they roped the cow and discovered that she was blind. With blindness her sense of smell was so keenly developed that she was able to follow her calf as it led her on the trails from grass to water.

If children had this much love and respect for their mothers, the world would be largely freed of crime and other social problems.

The cow earned a retirement on greener pastures.

The Soft Spot

The dude came out of Texas and worked in security at a Hughes's hotel. He was tall and mean-looking. His disposition seemed to fit his looks. His vocabulary was limited, so he had to shim it up with a lot of cusswords. His feet ran out along the ground an unusual distance, but they were not out of proportion to his long legs.

Jim said to Kim, "You'd better give this dude a tall horse to ride or his feet will drag on the ground. Perhaps Eagle would be suitable."

This hard-looking, tough-talking dude was just the kind of cowboy needed to try his skill with the Conway bulls on the Conway Ranch, which Hughes had bought.

Nevertheless, even the toughest and the meanest have some weaknesses and soft spots that are thoroughly camouflaged.

At breakfast the dude bragged about what he would do when he roped a wild bull.

After a parting cup of coffee, the cowboys mounted their horses. The dude put his left foot in the stirrup, and as he did so, Eagle stepped on the toes of the dude's right foot. With a foot in the stirrup and the other on the ground under Eagle's hoof, the dude was pinned halfway between the saddle and

Jim Haworth drawing, "Leading the Blind."

Jim Haworth drawing, "Heading for the High Country."

the ground. He let out a bellow that would have frightened a tame bull and yelled, "Get this damn horse off my toe!"

He was rescued, but old Eagle had found his soft spot. The dude didn't ride; he went back to town.

A Hughes Cowboy Camp: Experiences of the Cowboys and Jim Haworth
by Lorin Bunker

There is literature written about Indian camps, scout camps, pioneer camps, and plain old prospector camps. However, none of these compared with or were as functional as Mr. Hughes's cowboy camp.

There is no one as lazy as a cowboy when he is in camp. Maybe it is not laziness, because the camp is only a place to eat and sleep and then leave again. A few rocks are put in a circle and the fire is built therein. Across the rocks is a screen and grill. Bacon and eggs and hotcakes are cooked on the grill, and the coffeepot has a resting place on the screen. Nearby on the ground is a pile of wood and a box of grub, or groceries.

The bedrolls are in a perimeter around the fire, and the cowboys recline against the same. The lone cedar tree is of no use for shade, as the cowboys are usually gone during daylight hours.

Dust and flies are camp followers, and the boiling sun is a purifier. The State Health Department never made an inspection, but no one died of ptomaine poisoning.

The Coffeepot

The coffeepot had seen better days, but that was a long

time ago. It wasn't a cast-off gift from the Desert Inn or, in fact, any of Mr. Hughes's hotels. It looked more like it came from a junkyard, but surely the empire would not condone robbing the trash pile.

Regardless of its looks, it was still in service. It had probably brewed over a thousand gallons of coffee over an equal number of campfires.

The inside of the pot was as black as the outside. There was no lid to keep out the dust and the ashes. The handle was broken off, and the spout was bent. The bail was gone and had been replaced with hay wire.

In answer to how the spout got bent, Jim replied, "One frosty morning I put a cold saddle on a bronco. When I got on, he bucked through the fire and kicked the coffeepot."

When asked when he was going to replace it, Jim answered, "It's good for a few more years. Our tight budget does not permit any extravagances. Besides, the cows don't know any difference."

The Far-Off Help

There were big plans when the empire went into the ranching business. Corrals were to be built, and the springs and water holes were to be developed.

Dreams and plans go astray when there are no finances to carry them out. It seems that there was a dire need and the hotels and casinos needed the ranch money.

At the White Rock Spring there was only a trickle of water. It seeped out from between the rocks and ran a few rods and disappeared in the sand.

Thirsty cows and horses came in from the range at all hours of the day and night. They contested for the water, and none of them left with its thirst fully quenched.

Jim would like to do better, and the BLM would help in part. But Howard and Annie (often called Wild Horse Annie, she was a well-known Eastern environmentalist) were not here and the Hughes empire was not interested. Maybe the Humane Society could help.

Of course the situation at White Rock Springs was no different now than it had been for a hundred years, so why worry?

The Baling Wire Ranch

In making the ranch a going concern, Jim suffered everything from frustrations to ulcers to broken bones. He loved the work but hated to borrow equipment from a poor neighbor when Hughes's equipment was broken down.

However, during many small emergencies, broken gates and equipment were patched up with baling wire. This wire served a double purpose. First it was tied around a bale of hay, then used for multiple purposes on the ranch. Wire became the repairer of the breach. Mr. Hughes should have been proud of his baling wire outfit.

This wire was used for most everything but shoelaces.

The Cook Turned Cowboy

At one time or another everyone wants to be a cowboy. Some have tried it and found that their fear overcame their courage.

The toughest broncs have been ridden on a barstool, and the drugstore cowboys far outnumber the real cowboys. These dudes were always pestering Jim to take them on a trip to the range.

One of these so-called dudes was a good cook from the Hughes Frontier Hotel, but only a fair cook out of a Dutch oven. However, the cowboys did not complain, as they would rather eat his grub than do the cooking themselves. Anyway, the dude was doing fairly well until he received a strong, uncontrollable desire to be a cowboy.

Jim knew argument was useless, so on the day of the big drive he let the cook ride Rhino. By midmorning the hair was rubbed off the cook's legs. By noon his legs were chafing, and the day was only half-gone. By midafternoon the dude was walking and leading Rhino. At sundown, Rhino came to camp leading the dude. The dude was hanging onto Rhino's tail.

Such is the history of a cook turned to cowboy and turned back into a cook in one day's time. He gave up the Dutch oven and the coffeepot for the protection of the union and the Frontier Hotel.

He never did thank Jim for allowing him to try out for a cowboy.

Iris

Jim's wife, Iris, is a petite, lovely lady with raven black hair and dark-lashed green eyes. They are knowing eyes that seem to take in a situation immediately that she may act on the same, if necessary, or quietly store the knowledge in her mind for future reference. She is indeed a helpmate and a companion to her husband.

Clint once asked, "Are you Indian?"

She said, "My father and grandfather were friends with the Indians. I had an uncle who was killed by an Indian. That was sad."

Clint was embarrassed by his attempt to compliment her.

The Hughes Warm Springs Ranch.

Her beautiful features and quickness had reminded him of his distant Seneca Indian background.

Through Jim and Iris's devotion they have never allowed other interests or the empire job to come between them.

When the empire hired Jim, they hired two employees for the price of one; Iris was the bonus. Iris kept the home fires burning, acting as a secretary, and enjoyed a ride on the range. She was often seen, in her ranch attire, riding in search of lost dogies.

Some of the empire's money lost in the hotels could better have been spent employing and appreciating Iris.

However, there is no way that love, loyalty, and service to the empire can be measured in compensation.

Jim Haworth drawing, "Iris Relaxing."

Dreams

It was on the Delamar flats and the cowboys were camped at the point of the Rocks Pond. The cowboys had retired, the horses were eating hay, a cow bawled for her calf, and a lonely coyote pointed his nose to the stars and howled.

It was under these conditions that Jim's weary body succumbed to slumber and his mind drifted away into those thoughts that come by night. Dreams fleetingly came and went, and then it seemed to him that the wealthy Mr. Hughes must be happy to be free of his empire, his poor health, greedy people, hotels, casinos, and cows.

The cold earth began to penetrate the warmth of Jim's bed, which was on the ground, and a chill went through his body. His dreams changed and he reflected on his own miserable condition.

Jim awoke when the Morning Star came over the horizon. He arose from his bed and dressed and walked in the desert under the light of a dawning day. In his meditations he analyzed his dreams, and though he could not interpret the exactness of their meaning, he knew that in the providence of God man does receive light and truth from Him.

Jim Haworth drawing, "Ridin' Dubble."

Loco Weed versus Marijuana

Men and animals share the same world and the same fate. There is a heaven for the critters of the range even as there is a heaven for men. The critters of the range manage their affairs according to instinct. Man is to use reason and intelligence; however, some people insist on living below the level of animals.

When the grass is short and the locoweed grows lush, some of the cows and horses will nibble at it because of their hunger. As the consumption of the weed increases, it affects their nervous system and they act strangely. When they cannot get their head down to drink then it will be only a short time before death overtakes them.

A man cannot blame his narcotic habits on short grass. His is a deliberate act that can bring him the same fate as a cow on locoweed, for with his acts comes a judgment.

As the Scriptures say:

> Be not deceived; for God is not mocked: for whatsoever a man soweth, that shall he also reap.
> For he that soweth to his flesh shall of his flesh reap corruption; but he that soweth to the Spirit shall of the Spirit reap life everlasting.

Thus, this is the lot of man.

Advantages of a Medicare Card

The evidence seemed to indicate that Mr. Hughes was a very sick man and that he was difficult to care for. The time of departure from this life comes at varied times and under many different circumstances. Mr. Hughes would probably have enjoyed better health and lived longer if he had had a Medicare card and had been able to use it.

However, he probably had no complaints, for he died in the sky, in his ears the drone of an airplane motor—which was his first love.

The Resting Place

A bunkhouse is just what it implies, a place to keep out of the wind, cook a meal, and lay a tired body on a bed.

Mr. Hughes's bunkhouse was not much better or worse than many others. It was not skillfully built, because the cowboys put it together in their spare time. The ranch budget had always been tight and the hotels couldn't afford to make a contribution for the construction, so the cowboys tore down an old building and sort of glued the bunkhouse together.

This bunkhouse was not the kind of a place that you would want to take your bride for a honeymoon. However, if you did, she would remember it for a long time.

The cupboard was empty, like grandmother Hubbard's, and the only cooking utensils were a coffeepot and frying pan.

However, Hughes's ranch bunkhouse did have hot and cold water, a shower, and an indoor toilet. The thing that was distinctive was the toilet. The seat was scarred, and the reservoir to hold the flushing water had no lid. After the flushing and when the overhead tank was refilling, there came from the refilling mechanism a spray of water, and if a cowboy lingered too long on the seat, he received a shower.

To control this the cowboys placed a pie plate over the spray to divert the water into the tank.

Now, Mr. Hughes never enjoyed anything like this. However, it was better than going to the brush for your morning's morning.

Now one complained; no one fixed it.

A Long Life Is Doubtful

Mr. Hughes's ranches and range rights covered areas larger than most counties. He never enjoyed life this side of his empire. The healing qualities of the wide open spaces would have prolonged his life. However, the life expectancy of Jim and Kim is not rated as being very long if they don't stop catching wild bulls. In fact, if the insurance company knew of their antics, they would raise the rate. It was said to Jim and Kim, "Why don't you slow down and live longer?"

Jim answered, "The work has to be done, and if a wild bull sends us to meet Mr. Hughes, I am sure that he will greet us cordially."

"And if this happens the empire will have to hire four men to take our place," added Kim.

Cowboy in a Pine-Nut Tree

Starlings in a cherry tree are as bad as squirrels in a nut tree—neither sight would compare with a cowboy in a pine nut tree. If Jim carried lunches for his cowboys, they wouldn't have to stop the roundup to pick nuts from a piñon tree to satisfy their hunger.

The tree wasn't too large to begin with, and it was loaded with pinecones that had just opened after the first hard frost. Two cowboys were in the tree, with their chaps on, shaking the cones and nuts to the ground. Three cowboys were on their hands and knees picking the nuts from the bed of pine needles.

An hour was spent picking and eating pine nuts, and as

they rode away munching on nuts, Jim said, "With that hour we spent picking pine nuts it's going to be difficult to get in a full twelve-hours working shift."

To which the cowboys replied, "If Hughes was here we would form a cowboy union for our personal protection."

Cowboys on Hughes's Ranch, 1978. From left to right: Riding Eagle, Newt Bundy; riding Quedo, Jim Haworth. Moving toward Grassie Spring, Oakspring allotment, Delamar Flats.

A Time of Confession

From the Scriptures it would appear that all sins must be confessed and all wrongs made right, whether it be in this life or the life hereafter. Mr. Hughes will undoubtedly have to patch up some broken fences, and he will have to reserve a lot of his heavenly time to listen to the confessions and apologies of the many that have taken advantage of him, whether it be the thieves or disloyal employees.

The Bulls Lock Horns

It was that time of the year when the cows had dropped their calves and the cowboys had an urge to raise another calf for Mr. Hughes. The bulls responded to this hereditary urge, willing to make their contribution toward another generation of calves.

With this urge the bulls responded to another instinct; every bull wanted to show his supremacy. When they came in from the range to the water hole there was a lot of bellowing and pawing of the earth as the bulls issued their challenge.

They were more fair in their battles than humans, for they did not gang up on each other. Each bull relied on his own strength and cunning.

The bulls fought among themselves, and the strongest challenged the leader. Thus it was that in their rage they pawed the earth, roared and bellowed, then with lowered head and arched neck charged at each other.

They tried to kill each other by bunting and gouging each other with their horns.

It was time for a cowboy to give them plenty of room. The cows and calves went on grazing, giving the battlers little of their attention, for regardless of the victor, it would bring no change in their lives.

The chief bulls in the Hughes empire were knocking heads and locking horns. Regardless of the outcome, hundreds of Hughes's lesser employees would go on about their duties, little affected by the outcome of the head honchos.

The Smell of the Buzzard

Buzzards are carrion eaters. They are as black as a blackbird and larger than a crow, with a head like a turkey. Their reputation is unsavory. Their vision is good, but their keenest instinct is their sense of smell. Their eyes can detect the faltering footsteps of the weak, but when the odor of approaching death comes to their nostrils they know that it is time to move in and take possession.

We called her Lola. She seemed to have the instincts of a buzzard. She didn't work, at least with her hands, and her charms were mostly ineffective. However, she had the smell of a buzzard and she could spot lonely old men that were on their last legs. Following her inclinations, she would move in with them, one by one, as a comforter, and when they died she would claim their meager possessions.

There were no heirs to object and the courts didn't mind, as there was not enough property to quarrel over. She earned what she got, and it was cheaper than putting them in a rest home or hospital, and to this extent the smell of the buzzard paid off and it saved the county some welfare expense.

During a lull in the run of the derelicts it appeared that Liz would have to go to work and she asked Jim for a job cooking for the cowboys. Jim was immediately concerned for his own health and the welfare of his cowboys, so he turned her down.

The Prize Stud and the Lowly Mustang

Zula was a black quarter horse with a blazed face. Mr. Hughes had never seen this prize stallion of his. It was really no one's fault when Zula left his easy life with the ranch mares and took to the hills. With his freedom on the range Zula had a desire to become a leader of a bunch of wild mares. To do this he would have to take them away from another stallion. There were plenty of wild horses, as they were wards of the government, and the opportunity soon came for him to fulfill his desires. Instinct told him that if he could whip or kill the other horse, the mares and foals would be his.

The Hughes stud was grain-fed and well groomed. The iron shoes on his feet would be to his advantage. He had a lot of courage but was short of experience.

With a whinny and a battle cry, Zula charged a smaller mustang stallion. They reared up and struck at each, then whirled and kicked. Charging each other again and again, they tried to kill or cripple by biting and kicking. They were soon flecked with bloody foam.

It seemed that the Hughes stud would win the battle, as his size and weight were forcing the mustang to retreat. However, the quickness and the cunning of the mustang soon put Zula to flight.

The Hughes stud was happy to return to the security of his own pasture.

The Hughes wealth was no match for the cunning of the mining mustangs.

Air Force Targets

If Mr. Hughes had spent his last days on the Delamar flats and surrounded himself with the normal comforts of life, his days would have been prolonged and been more enjoyable. Jim and Kim are fairly good horse doctors, and they could have taken good care of him. However, better than the physical nursing would have been the mental stimulation that would come from the whine of the low-flying air force fighter planes.

The air force used the Delamar area as a training area for

their pilots. They would fly up and down that country at ground level faster than the speed of sound. The cows had finally gotten used to the passing planes and quit stampeding. The sturdy old Joshua trees continued to tremble from the vibrations.

In these flights the pilots could knock a cowboy's hat off his head, so they should be able to stroke a trench with accurate gunfire.

Mr. Hughes would have thrived under these conditions and could have possibly invested something to protect the cowboys or help the air force.

Socks in the Grave

When the winter wind comes out of the north and blows through the Joshuas in the Delamar flats it don't have to howl at ninety miles an hour or be forty degrees below zero to chill a poor cowboy through and through.

After a few days of this and after a few nights in a cold bed cowboys begin to wonder what happened to last summer's wages. The dudes don't come out of the Hughes hotels to play cowboy at these times.

"These are the times that try men's souls." Do they want to be a cowboy or a crap dealer? The choice has been made, as the cowboy doubles up on all his clothing and ties his bandanna across his face and over his ears to protect them from the biting cold.

Kim was not much to complain, but occasionally he would get off his horse and walk to warm up his feet. However, he did say, "Listen one and listen all. When I die I want two pair of heavy wool socks put on my feet. I don't want any cold feet while I am in the grave."

Such Tender Care

In reading reports of Mr. Hughes one learns that he let his hair and beard grow long, also his fingernails and toenails. Apparently his aides did not raise too much objection to his looks and habits for fear of being ostracized from his good graces and payroll.

There must have been times when Mel Steward longed to get at Mr. Hughes with his barber tools, but there may have been other barriers than just Mr. Hughes. It seemed that Mr. Hughes was well groomed when he was visited by the governor of Nevada. However, the sketches of him that appear in the press reflect him as being shaggy-headed. Apparently Mr. Hughes had his phobias and peculiar traits and through the years these things became more exaggerated, until by the time of his death they had taken him away from his normal self.

A Government Error: Wild Horse Annie

The Howard R. Hughes cowboys respected the laws of the land, even though they were tempted to rope a wild horse. The horses and deer protected by the law were gentler than the wild cattle. Many times when chasing wild cattle the cowboys would ride through a band of horses or herd of deer.

To keep nature in balance, everything has to have its opposite, such as the grass, the jackrabbit, and the coyote. But man doesn't need an opposite; he can destroy himself fast enough.

Wild Horse Annie felt that the wild horses and jackasses needed government protection. As a result of her pressure, the jackasses in Washington passed a law to protect the horses and burros. Now the horses and burros have become so numerous they are a nuisance. The cowboy was part of the ecology to control the horse and jackass population, but the government put them afoot.

The cougar likes the law, as it reserves more horsemeat for him. The bones of colts glisten in the sun; the meat thereof went to feed the hungry cats.

Annie and Howard are up yonder and they can talk it over and see if there is a better way to handle the horse and donkey problem created by the government. Of course, their decisions won't affect the problem.

Jim Haworth drawing, "Gold Butte's Wild Burrow."

The Catastrophe

The herd had been gathered, and they were headed toward the corral. The Indian boy mounted on Brownie was bringing up the drag. A big red line-backed cow kept cutting from the herd and heading towards the hills. Being short-handed, the Indian boy couldn't spend all his time with one cow so he decided to teach her a lesson.

With a doubled rope and at a high gallop he taught that cow a lesson. However, in so doing, Brownie stepped into a badger hole and fell to the ground. The Indian was thrown head over heels and landed in a pile of rocks; fortunately, his only injury was a broken arm.

The horse sluggishly got up, but the next morning he was dead.

Jim Haworth drawing, "Stampede at Juanita Springs."

The Sound of Music, the Taste of Dust

It was branding and weaning time on unit seven. With some extra cowboys and the barking of dogs, about five hundred head of cattle were headed toward the grassy corral and water hole.

Calves were bawling for their mothers, and the mothers were mooing for their calves. Dogs were barking and cowboys were yelling as they galloped on tired cow ponies. The sound was more pleasant and satisfying than the music of the orchestra at the Sands Hotel.

A blanket of thick dust covered the scene and Kim, riding in the dust, said, "I will always be a valuable employee; even when I am old and blind I will be able to tell what part of Mr Hughes's range I am on by the taste and smell of the dust."

The Hughes Curtain

The little Dutch boy found a hole in the dike and put his finger in it until help came to repair the leak. He could have become a national hero for saving Holland from being flooded.

Jim saw where the Hughes empire had sprung a leak. He put his finger in the hole and then his arm, but no help came to shut off the flow of money that was disappearing.

Going over the heads of authorized agents, Jim called directly to the inner sanctum located in California to talk to the head man. The best he cold do was to get an underling, who indicated that Mr. Gay would call him.

As of yet Jim hasn't received the call.

The Iron Curtain and the Bamboo Curtain are nothing compared with the inner sanctum security of the Hughes empire.

Jim Haworth drawing of bucking horse.

Jim Haworth drawing, "Bringin' in a Wild One."

Mr. Hughes had been in isolation so long it is doubtful that Gay would have been let into the inner sanctum.

The Hungry Cougar

Even after the colt was gone, the mare, for several days, kept returning to the place they had last been together. While there she whinnied for her colt, but there was no answer. The mare never stayed long because the odor of cat was strong and she was nervous.

The cougar was old, his claws were dull, and his teeth were broken. His days as a powerful hunter were over. His preference was horsemeat, but now and then he had to settle for a calf of Mr. Hughes.

The trails to and from the watering place went through groves of cedar and pine trees. The cat would lay on the limb of a tree that the trail went under and spring down on an unsuspecting colt. It was always a young animal, for the cat never had the strength to tackle a big horse.

After the kill the cougar had to find another limb in the right place on another trail.

The government trapper had never informed the cat that it was against the law to kill horses.

Jim Haworth drawing, "Mother's Love."

11
Paranoia in the Seventies

The 1970s were years of stressful events closing in on Howard Hughes's paranoid life.

To get the U.S. attorney general's approval of his purchase of the Dunes Hotel and Casino, Howard Hughes became deeply involved in President Nixon's machine.

First, there was a matter of $100,000 from Howard Hughes to Richard Nixon's reelection campaign. Because of a clerical error in the Dunes value to the tune of an increase of several million dollars, the deal fell through. Therefore, the $100,000 was resting in safekeeping with Bebe Rebozo, Nixon's manager. It was not used in the campaign. This and other Nixon-Hughes capers and Nixon's family side deals fouled up the Hughes purchase of Air West Airlines. Evidence of these deals was in files of the Democratic National Committee. These incidents became principal issues of the ill-fated Watergate break-in.

By buying favors from Nixon, Howard Hughes was trying to protect Las Vegas from the rampant underworld and gambling to increase and protect his own empire. Also, the danger of pending underground nuclear tests nearby worried Hughes. He was determined to prevent underground nuclear testing in Nevada, at any cost. The handling of his deals was passed around various agencies and government officials where each had his cut. Hughes's secret contributions to

President Nixon's campaign were known by the Democratic campaign manager, Lawrence O'Brien, who also, at the same time, worked for Hughes. That information was kept in Democratic Party files. It would be damaging to Howard Hughes and President Nixon should it be revealed. President Nixon's campaign managers, concerned that the Democratic National Committee might release the information, staged the Watergate break-in. None of this common spying by underlings on each other in business or politics seems to be ample reason to cause a President of the United States to resign or be impeached. History reveals worse antics by many former presidents or their party.

The Ouster of Maheu and Replacement with Gay

Late in 1970, Bill Gay hired Robert Peloquin (PI) to separate Maheu from Howard Hughes. While Hughes was in his worst depressive state, Gay fed him information that Maheu was stealing from all areas of the Hughes Nevada operations, of which Robert Maheu was president.

Maheu, disappointed with Hughes attorney Chester C. Davis and Bill Gay's handling of the still-pending TWA case (after Hughes sold his shares of TWA, he still had a judgment of $150,000,000 against him for fraud and mishandling of Air West stock), dismissed Davis and Gay. Bill Gay, jealous and worried about Maheu's power with Hughes and exposure of his own misdealings, finally "poisoned" Howard Hughes's confidence in Maheu to the point that Hughes condemned Maheu as a crooked bastard and signed an order on December 3, 1970, firing Maheu. This prompted Bob Maheu on January 1, 1972, to file a $17,500,000 slander, libel, and damages suit against Howard Hughes. The deposition was not taken until July 1973, a year and a half later.

After Maheu's firing, Larry O'Brien, head of the Democratic National Committee, was Hughes's watchdog in the U.S. Congress, there to inform Hughes of pending tax and antitrust proceedings. O'Brien was at the same time head of the Democratic National Committee.

Howard Hughes had for years tried desperately to use his wealth to stop underground nuclear testing in Nevada. He gave $50,000 cash here and there to vice presidents, presidents, and others. He had made bad business deals with Nixon's brother, Don, and with Nixon. It was no wonder President Nixon wanted all the information possible from the files of the Democratic National Committee pertaining to his questionable activities.

Despite no lack of wide Watergate publicity, Howard Hughes was hardly mentioned as a key figure. However, had he not been involved, there probably would not have been a Watergate. Had the caper not been the plan of top political figures, it probably would have been reported as another example of Howard Hughes's high finance for what he considered a national emergency. Howard Hughes never voted and never would run for a public office. His political interest was to protect his own well-being, his health, his wealth, and his country. As always, no matter how silent, money does talk. Howard Hughes was a poor listener. He was hard of hearing from birth, the reason he only heard what he tuned in to, as do other hard-of-hearing people. He did not wear a hearing aid. He made his own slow decisions in his dome of silence. Had he listened to Robert Maheu, he probably would have saved his sanity.

The Glomar II Incident and Watergate

In 1970, the CIA, for some unknown reason, decided it

Frank William (Bill) Gay, Hughes's personal staff director at Romaine. *(Wide World Photos)*

wanted to raise a sunken, outdated Soviet submarine. The project was code-named Project Jennifer. Global Marine was selected to special-fit one of its deep-sea oil drilling ships for the three-mile plunge into the briny deep. To avoid public scrutiny, considerable publicity was released by the CIA that Howard Hughes was outfitting the ship to search for riches on the sea bottom. Howard Hughes actually was using this CIA contract to aid in his dream of undersea exploration.

Howard Hughes was interested because he really thought he could invent equipment to mine precious metals on the deep-sea floor, thus make a good profit for himself and satisfy the CIA, by raising the sunken ship. He called the expedition ship *Glomar II*. Five hundred million dollars was furnished by the CIA (taxpayers' money). Howard Hughes was paid to research and develop the equipment for Global Marine to build the vessel.

The ill-fated break-in at Hughes's 7000 Romaine Street, Los Angeles, and stealing of Hughes's confidential files caused the cancellation of the *Glomar* ship project and exposure of the CIA's intentions. It was an investment in a pipe dream of the CIA, but a real dream of Howard Hughes that could have produced another addition of wealth and simultaneously satisfy the billionaire's concern for conservation, the environment, and the health and well-being of Americans.

The hidden CIA contract was in the 7000 Romaine Street safe, but the Nixon executives thought it was in the Democratic National Committee's file. Then Nixon as well as the CIA would be blamed for the *Glomar II* failure. Since Howard Hughes had the CIA contract, he was knowingly a party to the dumb scandal that, in part, caused Richard Nixon to resign from the presidency of the United States.

The project was a secret mission ordered by the CIA, and it was felt that exposure of the mission would aggravate U.S.–Soviet relations. The principal purpose of the Watergate break-in was, however, to recover additional information the Democratic National Committee was going to use to discredit Nixon for the $100,000 and other gifts he had received from Hughes.

From 1971 to 1974, the Hughes Aircraft Company, owned by the Howard Hughes Institute (a nonprofit charity), guaranteed loans for superdevelopment of the Marina del Rey apartments and club. President Nixon was coinvestor through his tax accountant and his law firm. For tax purposes, the luxury development showed large financial losses. In 1974 alone, it lost $9,165,228. The tax returns were prepared by Nixon's own tax accountant. Then Howard Hughes, through his tax-exempt Howard Hughes Medical Institute, actually financed the huge project, and every dollar invested was tax-exempt.

December 7, 1971, the Clifford Michael Irving hoax was history. Howard Hughes's famous last public meeting (a telephone conversation) with the press, was held January 7, 1972. Hughes was now showing poor memory and couldn't remember General George worked for him in his Hughes Electronics firm.

Howard Hughes's biggest blunder was during his last sinking into manic depression when he said, "Maheu stole me blind. He's a no-good dishonest son of a bitch." This statement caused Maheu to, on February 10, 1972, file a $17,500,000 slander suit. It was overturned December 27, 1977, and finally an unknown amount determined in an out-of-court settlement was given to Maheu.

The Big Giveaway: Sale of Hughes Tool Company

September 3, 1972, Raymond Holliday signed documents in Houston to establish a new Hughes Tool Company.

Robert A. Maheu, chief of Hughes's Nevada operations. *(United Press International)*

Howard Hughes's deteriorating mental condition was seized by William Gay as an opportunity to take over Howard Hughes Enterprises. Gay arranged for Hughes to escape to the Bahamas, where the most devastating events were arranged by Gay and his Mormon aides. In Howard Hughes's mental state, he was happy to arrive in the Bahamas hotel Zanu Princess. Without knowledge of Gay's plans, he busied himself with plans to buy the Bahamas.

In the Bahamas, though suffering from deep depression and ever-increasing doses of cocaine and other addictives, Howard Hughes was determined to buy the Bahama islands. When he was thwarted by the Bahamian government he returned to Miami, then went on to Nicaragua.

During Howard Hughes's off-and-on three-year stay in the Bahamas, his hold on Hughes Tool Company came in jeopardy.

After the Gay aides settled Howard Hughes in his penthouse suite of the Bahamian Hotel Zanu Princess, William Gay's activity began in earnest to sell Hughes's father's Hughes Tool Company and its subsidiaries.

Hughes and the IRS were fed information of huge losses in his Las Vegas hotels and casinos while all the other Las Vegas casinos and hotels were showing huge profits. Bill Gay claimed to Howard Hughes that Maheu had stolen the profits. This plus facing the huge Air West lawsuit made Hughes desperate for funds. Although he did not want to sell Hughes Tool Company, he was in no physical or mental condition to resist. Raymond Holliday, his Houston chief executive of Hughes Tool Company, Hughes's attorney Chester Davis, and William Gay engineered the public sale of all of Hughes Tool Company stock (100 percent belonging to Howard Hughes). When the public sale was ready, Holliday presented the documents to Howard Hughes for his signature.

On September 13, 1972, Raymond Holliday signed the documents to sell Hughes Tool Company and establish a new public-owned Hughes Tool Company. Hughes had wanted to hold off until 1973, but Holliday convinced him he must sell now. On December 7, 1972, seventeen days before Hughes's seventieth birthday, all of the Hughes Tool Company stock was sold for $30 per share, bringing Howard Hughes $150,000,000, less costs.

The new Hughes Tool Company automatically became the Summa Corporation along with Hughes's hotels, casinos, and all Nevada operations: the Las Vegas TV station, Air West, Hughes Sports Network, the Helicopter Manufacturing Company, the undeveloped land, etc. No mention was made of the Hughes Warm Springs empire. However, Gay assumed control until Hughes died.

Howard Hughes was out of Hughes Tool Company and all its subsidiaries.

Even in Howard Hughes's darkest moments, he seemed to know he should wait a year before selling out. The oil tool business had been in a slump but showed signs of a profit for the 1972 year. He was right. The stock he sold for $30 a share December 7, 1971, rebounded to $90 a share by 1972 year's end. In fact, during the next five years, the oil tool division's net income was $162.5 million, $12 million more than Hughes received for his entire holdings.

Also, in 1973, the Air West judgment against Howard Hughes was canceled. He would not have needed to sell Hughes Tool Company.

In 1970, Howard Hughes lost his power to buy and control. His attempt to buy the Bahamas islands failed. This abruptly ended Howard Hughes's self-esteem and confidence and will to proceed with his life. His paranoia deepened, and his drug addiction accelerated. He had lost control of his empire and he lost the experience and abilities of his alter ego when he lost his man, Robert Aime Maheu, the man who made Howard Hughes's wishes come true.

February 15, 1972, after Howard Hughes's Bahamas disappointment, he traveled by boat to Miami, from where he flew to Nicaragua, then to Canada, then returned to Nicaragua. In Nicaragua, on September 25, 1972, he was coerced into signing away his entire empire.

On December 7, Pearl Harbor Day, the sale took place. All of the stock (Howard Hughes's) was sold at a price of $30 per share, giving Howard Hughes a paltry $150 million (less expenses) for his billion-dollar empire.

On December 24 (Christmas Eve), 1972, Howard Hughes was flown to London to the Inn at the Park. He was determined to pilot a plane for the last time, much against the advice of airport officials. He finally obtained an airplane and pilot and did pilot the plane for a short run. He managed to temporarily handle the controls and pilot the plane around London.

January 10, 1973, Howard Hughes received the good news that the TWA judgment against him was overturned by the U.S. Supreme Court.

December 23, a year after arriving in London, he was flown back to the Bahamas.

In January 1974, Howard Hughes received the good news that the Air West indictment was dismissed.

The true *Glomar II* story has been revealed. February 10, 1975, Howard Hughes was flown on his last trip to Nicaragua. During his miserable month in Nicaragua before his death, he was subjected to more and more narcotics. His whole body deteriorated to a point where he became comatose. He was flown to Acapulco, Mexico, where doctors were unable to revive him, and his doctor, Wilbur Thain of Ogden, Utah, was summoned. He refused to attend Howard Hughes this last time. He said he was leaving on a vacation.

In Acapulco, Howard Hughes was carried to an airplane where he died en route to Houston on April 5, 1976.

The Hughes Estate

After Howard Robard Hughes's death on April 5, 1976, much has been written and refuted concerning the legalities and claims to the Howard Hughes fortune.

Howard Hughes on his deathbed mumbled about his will. With feeble gestures he was trying to indicate his concern with the loss of wills. In all his handwritten wills he stated that his Aunt Annette and her son, William R. Lummis, were his principal concern and that he entrusted the will to the safety of the First National Bank in Nevada. Aunt Annette guarded and managed him after his father's death. He used the First National Bank of Nevada as depository for his last will and for the gold bars from his mines, deposited there by Jim Haworth and Francis Fillerup.

When cousin William R. Lummis was named coexecutor with the bank by the court, he moved to the Desert Inn penthouse suite in Las Vegas and operated the business of the estate as Howard Hughes would have wanted.

William Lummis, a prominent Houston lawyer in his own right, deftly eliminated the control of Hughes's Nevada operation. His first order of business was meeting with, and firing of, Bill Gay. Then Lummis visited Jim Haworth at the ranch empire. With no knowledge of ranch management, he called Jim to his Las Vegas office for consultations. As he learned more of Jim's dedication to Howard Hughes, they became good friends.

Iris Haworth relates how William Lummis seemed to arrange his visits to the ranch to coincide with cowboy lunchtime. Consulting with Jim, William Lummis listed the Hughes Warm Springs Ranch for sale. A listing price of $8,075,000 was decided. As of October 12, 1977, he also authorized a salary increase to $20,000 per year for Jim and sold the ranch to LDS for $4.5 million.

Dear Mr McKay
please see that this Will
is delivered after my death to
Clark County Court House
Las Vegas Nevada
          Howard R. Hughes
    Last Will and Testament

    I Howard R. Hughes ------ of
sound and disposing mind and
memory, not acting under duress
fraud or the undue influence
of any person whomsoever,
and being a resident of Las Vegas
Nevada, declare that this
is to be my last Will
and revoke all other wills
previously made by me —
    After my death my estate
is to be devided as follows

first one forth of all my as-
    sets to go to Hughes Med-
    ical Institute of Miami —
second: one eight of assets
    to be devided among
    The University of Texas —
    Rice Institute of Technology

One of Contested Wills

of Houston
the University of Nevada
and the University of Calif.
                              Howard R. Hughes
— page one —

third: one sixteenth to Church
of Jesus Christ of Latter-day
Saints — David O. Mackay- Pre

Forth: one sixteenth to establish a home for Orphan
Cildren —

Fifth: one sixteenth of assets
to go to Boy Scouts
of America -

sixth: one sixteenth; to be
divided among Jean Peters of
Los Angeles and Ella Rice
of Houston —

seventh: one sixteenth of assets
to William R. Lommis of
Houston, Texas —

eighth: one sixteenth to go
to Pigelvin Du Mar of
Gabbs Nevada —

                    Howard R Hughs
— page two —

Ninth: one sixteenth to be devided among my personal aids at the time of my death —

tenth: one sixteenth to be used as school scholarship fund for entire Country —

The spruce goose is to be given to the City of Long Beach, Calif.

The remainder of my estate is to be devided among the key men of the company I own at the time of my death.

I appoint Noah Dietrich as the executer of this Will —

signed the 19 day of March 1968

Howard R. Hughes

— page Three —

Author's note: There are several spelling errors not characteristic of Howard Hughes.

After several interesting offers to purchase the ranch, the LDS in Salt Lake City, Utah, offered the low price of $4.5 million.

William Lummis conferred with Jim. He said, "Jim, what do you think of selling the ranch to the Mormon church?"

Jim piped up, "Their money is as good as anyone's." For Jim, a rancher of few emotions, this was a good response.

Lummis said, "What about you? I don't want you dismissed from the empire. You are my ranch executive."

Jim replied, "I never will stop ranching. Iris and I are good Mormons. I would be satisfied to work for the church."

Lummis inserted a condition in the sale that Jim Haworth would continue as Hughes's Warm Springs Ranch manager for $20,000 a year for as long as he desired.

The Hughes Warm Springs Ranch was sold to LDS on January 31, 1978.

 Ranching Division

Post Office Box 309
Las Vegas, Nevada 89101
702 735 9182

A Division of
Summa Corporation

WARM SPRINGS AND CONAWAY RANCHES

LOCATION:	In Clark and Lincoln Counties, Nevada.
	In the upper Moapa Valley - Meadow Valley, Delamar Mountains, Delamar Valley and Gold Butte.
HEADQUARTERS:	Warm Springs Ranch, Moapa, Nevada.
OPERATION:	The Warm Springs and Conaway ranches operate as a single unit. Livestock and grazing rights have been commingled. Purebred herds and fat cattle feeding are maintained at Warm Springs. Range cattle and weanlings are handled at Conaway.

SIZE:

Deeded	2,720 acres, plus
B.L.M.	694,667 acres ±
National Park Land (used but not under contract)	200,000 acres ±
Total.	897,387 acres ±

CARRYING CAPACITY: (Approximately)

Warm Springs Ranch	1,100 head year-round
Conaway Ranch	700 head year-round
Range - 23,182 active A.U.M.s	2,200 head year-round
Total.	4,000 head year-round

PRICE: $8,075,000 for both ranches. However, will consider separate offers.

TERMS: CASH OR NEGOTIABLE

ENCUMBRANCES: NONE

Sale of Warm Springs Ranch to Church of Jesus Christ of Latter-Day Saints, January 31, 1978.

William R. Lummis, Hughes's first cousin and son of Annette Lummis, the heir around whom other family members united after Hughes's death. *(Wide World Photos)*

August 11, 1995

Jim Haworth
Moapa NV

My Dear Friend Jim,

    My memory takes me back to the hills in the Riggs area where we were meeting with some success in catching wild cattle. We were working for a boss that we had never met. He was Howard Hughes. It was hard work with long hours in a rough country. We had some reason to complain, for we were not getting paid as much as a shill would at a crap table.

    However, we looked toward the boss with some sympathy, because rumor had it that physically he was not faring too well. As we reasoned together, we felt that if he came to the hills to help us, his health would improve and we could give him better care and attention than he could receive from his palace guards that labored for money.

    Anyway Jim, it is a long story and you know it well. In roping wild cattle, you know well the dangers to life and limb, to both man and horse. During this period of time I began to record the incidents that took place. These recordings eventually found their way into a book compiled by Clint Baxter entitled "Howard Hughes: The Other Empire and His Man."

    Jim, you can act with whatever freedom you need to satisfy the needs of the author and publisher. I would rather take them on a wild ride down a rocky ridge among the cedars after a long horned cow. It would be more to my liking and their understanding.

    Jim, we wish you and Iris every success.

                              Very Truly Yours,

                              Lorin & Thelma Bunker

                              Lorin and Thelma Bunker

Epilogue

Howard Hughes, through inherent masterful thinking and fearless perseverance and hard work, demonstrated his oneness and manic depression. He emulated his father's determined characteristics and his mother's concern for his health. His San Limbo was time for the best uninterrupted plans for his singular accomplishments.

In his own way he sought and paid dearly for personal protection from human and biological vermin. In his own words, "The thing to love most is the land, the sea, the air and all the resources of nature."

He was a loyal American to the extreme and to his own detriment. He was not a gambler. He only pursued a goal with the self-assurance that he would win.

In the cracking of his super mental and physical strength, all psychological and physical systems went in uncontrolled reverse.

He demanded the best, whether it be beautiful women, building his own airplane and flying it around the world in record time, buying land to protect the environment, and influencing presidents and world leaders for the sake of humanity and nature. In spite of his critics, he reached every goal, though several times nearly killing himself. His goal to own his own beautiful natural oasis was reached but never fully enjoyed due to his untimely death.

The most revered possession, his Warm Springs other empire, was kept secret from the public and was held until he died. He singularly loved himself, his two wives, his land, and its natural resources and animals.

Howard Hughes's fame is for his determination. He never worried about the financial cost, whether for business or for pleasure.

He would be proud to know that his Hughes Warm Springs empire became the property of the LDS church of Salt Lake City, Utah.

His founding and endowment of his Howard Hughes Medical Research Institute through the initial gift of the famous Hughes Aircraft Company is a lasting memorial to Howard Robard Hughes.

Conclusion

Guided by the stewardship of James Haworth, the legacy of Howard Hughes's lifelong interest in environment ecology was and still is preserved on the Hughes Warm Springs, Nevada, Ranch.

After the purchase of the Hughes Warm Springs Ranch by the LDS church of Salt Lake City, Utah, on January 31, 1978, Jim Haworth continued as manager for five years, then, to date of this writing, leased the ranching division. He has maintained the water resources and the environment and continues to raise, break, and ride one hundred fine paint horses. He harvests his own hay and wrangles 200 head of cattle.

Postscript: Haworth Carries On the Hughes Dream and Warm Springs Ranch after Hughes

Concern for Jim Haworth after the sale of the Hughes

Jim and Iris Haworth enjoying ranching.

Warm Springs Ranch prompted William R. Lummis to include a provision of $25,000 per year for Jim's ranch management, which the LDS church readily accepted. The Church leases the water rights to Nevada Light and Power Company for $400,000 a year.

Jim and Iris work the ranch from their adjacent home and ranch. Jim continues his horse breeding program, training and promoting them to national rodeo championships.

In 1989, Jim and Iris celebrated their fiftieth wedding anniversary.

Jim continues serving on the board of directors of the Clark County Fair and the Nevada Ranchers' Association and

Jim and Iris celebrating their fiftieth wedding anniversary.

consultant with the Nevada Water Resources and Conservation Department.

When any Nevada rancher calls for help, Jim is there.

On request from the U.S. Department of Immigration's Mounted Border Patrol, Clint furnished his black horses and assistance in deterring nocturnal immigration of illegal aliens at the California-Mexico border.

In 1992 Clint Baxter moved his registered Blackjack Black Morgan horses to the Hughes Warm Springs Ranch under the care of Jim Haworth. At that time Jim proposed that his book, *Howard Hughes's Other Empire,* and his ranch drawings be

Howard Hughes's and Jim Haworth's concern for environment and ecology and love of nature and its potential lives on at the Hughes Warm Springs Ranch in the beautiful Moapa Valley of Nevada.

Silver Buckle Award, Clark County Fair. Front row, left to right: Glen Hardy, executive director; Jim Haworth; Iris Haworth; Jerry Haworth. Jerry, son of Jim and Iris, was director of the livestock show for many years.

combined with Clint's *Life of Howard Hughes* into the present book, *Howard Hughes, His Other Empire and, His Man.*

Clint lived with his wife, Helen Baxter, in Hesperia, California. He recently passed away.

Horse from the book *Blackjackshales Nightmares,* Clint Baxter.

Both Clint and Jim are of the Howard Hughes generation, and through Jim's entire life, after the age of twelve, he worked the Warm Springs Ranch in the Moapa Valley of Nevada. Clint's early life and during World War II was on a farm near Endicott, New York. Together, the authors wrote the book while working on the Howard Hughes Warm Springs ranch.

Jim Haworth states, "Howard Hughes would still be living if I could have gotten him here in his ranch and mansion paradise."